Plato, Ellen Francis Mason

A Day in Athens with Socrates

Translations from the Protagoras and the Republic of Plato

Plato, Ellen Francis Mason

A Day in Athens with Socrates
Translations from the Protagoras and the Republic of Plato

ISBN/EAN: 9783337005559

Printed in Europe, USA, Canada, Australia, Japan

Cover: Foto ©Thomas Meinert / pixelio.de

More available books at **www.hansebooks.com**

A DAY IN ATHENS

WITH SOCRATES

TRANSLATIONS

FROM

THE PROTAGORAS AND THE REPUBLIC

OF

PLATO

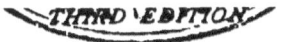

NEW YORK
CHARLES SCRIBNER'S SONS
1884

COPYRIGHT, 1883, BY
CHARLES SCRIBNER'S SONS.

Franklin Press:
RAND, AVERY, AND COMPANY,
BOSTON.

PREFACE.

These dialogues have been brought together, not with the idea that they will afford any adequate conception of Plato's philosophy, — the outgrowth of the teachings of Socrates, — but because they embody one of the most vivid pictures which have come down to us of the age in which these men lived and taught. It would be hard, indeed, to find a more perfect illustration of the distinctive characteristics of any age than is contained in the dialogues of Plato. Painter and poet no less than philosopher, he borrows colour from the scenes which surround him, and finds voice for his loftiest theories in the conversations of the men with whom he is in daily intercourse. As we follow the drama enacting before us, we feel that the lapse of centuries forms no barrier between that age and our own. Only when the action is set aside for the extended consideration of some abstract theme, are we made aware that our want of familiarity with the intellectual standpoint of that day too often proves an obstacle to a clear apprehension of the argument. Some of these difficulties may perhaps best be met by a glance at the position occupied by the newer schools of philosophy in relation to those that had gone before.

In earlier ages, intent upon examining "things under the earth and in the heavens,"[1] philosophers seem habitually to have withdrawn themselves to solitary heights of specula-

[1] Apology, 19 B.

tive thought, whence, to use Plato's words, "they look down with exceeding contempt upon us common men, and make but small account of us; nor even when they hold discourse do they take thought whether we keep pace with them or are left behind: each man of them goes on his own way."[1]

But the day was at hand when "common men" would no longer submit to entire exclusion from the world of philosophy. By this time, however, the inadequacy of systems which strove to "explain the unexplainable" had become but too apparent. An inevitable re-action took place in favour of the practical; and, answering to the new requirements of the day, a new school arose, which proclaimed the instruction of men in the right conduct of life as its chief end and purpose, and cultivated the arts of rhetoric and argumentation, which were yet novelties, as a help towards the attainment of this end.

It is easy to see, that to the active and subtle Greek mind, studies such as these would offer a peculiar attraction, and, pursued with a dangerous facility, might prove fatal to the end which they were at first intended to serve. "The Greek," says Taine, "is a reasoner even more than a metaphysician or a *savant*. He takes pleasure in delicate distinctions, in subtle analyses. He delights in splitting hairs, in weaving spiders' webs. In this his dexterity is unrivalled. Little matters it to him, that, alike in theory and in practice, this too-complicated and fine-drawn web is of no use whatever: he is content to watch the separate threads as they weave themselves into imperceptible and symmetrical meshes. Here the national vice is a final outcome of the national talent. Nowhere else has been seen a group of eminent and popular men who taught with success and

[1] Sophist, 243 A.

glory, as did Gorgias, Protagoras, and Polus, the art of making the worse appear the better cause, and maintained with an appearance of truth an absurd proposition, however shocking it might be." [1]

Ethical problems, to solve which was the avowed object of this new school of philosophy, but too frequently were abandoned for a training intended to ensure worldly success and fame; high ideals, sometimes even moral standards, were practically ignored; ability in discussion, facility of expression, came to be regarded not merely as helps to reach truth, but as the sole end of education, the "greatest good of man." [2] It is doubtless true that to class all the immediate predecessors of Socrates indiscriminately in one school is as unfair as to make their supposed method a mere synonyme for specious argument. Also in their favour it should be remembered that an inestimable service was rendered by these men in preparing the ground for Socrates himself, and through him for all subsequent philosophers. Had the doctrine that "Man is the measure of all things" not been proclaimed by Protagoras, the conclusion would less soon have been reached, that not only is philosophy made for man, but that man also is made for philosophy; and that hence his bounden duty, nay, his privilege it is, to apply to each act of his life the test whereby the true may be separated from the false, the real from the unreal.

But between the teachings of these men and those of Socrates there is a wide divergence — one less of degree than of kind, less of method than of aim and purpose. The long-winded harangues of other teachers, their confident dogmatism which induced an uncriticising acquiescence on the part of their pupils, differed indeed radically

[1] Taine, Philosophie de l'Art en Grèce, pp. 25, 26.   [2] Gorgias, 452 D.

from that rigid cross-examination in the light of which the confusion and poverty of thought hitherto covered by pompous fluency of diction were laid bare, and the listener was compelled to give an account of his real opinions, and either to substantiate or abandon them. Not until Socrates had "called down philosophy from the clouds,"[1] was the truth discerned that the work of self-examination is no vicarious task, but that to study and find out of what use you can be to men — in a word, to "know thyself"— is the study of studies, to last as long as a man shall live.[2]

In the pages before us we find the account given by Socrates of two famous conversations, — one between himself and Protagoras at the house of Callias, the other on the occasion of a visit to the venerable Cephalus and his household. It is surely no fanciful parallel which may be traced between the character of the dialogues themselves and the atmosphere of the households in which they took place. The bustle and confusion which already at break of day reign in the home of Callias offer a striking contrast with the repose and calm which in the evening hour, symbolic of the evening of his declining years, pervade the well-ordered abode of Cephalus; the pressing insistence with which Socrates is detained by the eager Callias well offsets the courteous dignity with which Cephalus invites him to be his frequent guest. But no less marked throughout is the contrast presented between the *Protagoras*, with its restless movement, its apparent absence of unity, and want of definite purpose, and the *Republic*, with its broad and stately sweep, its calm deliberateness of aim. Yet the one is the fitting precursor of the other; if in the second we find

---

[1] Cic. Tusc. Disp. V. iv. 10.
[2] See Xen. Mem. IV. ii. 24–30, and Apology, 38 A.

the perfect growth, in the first we have the promise of fruition. On purely artistic grounds, however, whether in point of vividness of colour or vivacity of action, it would be difficult to assign preference to one of these brilliant word-pictures over the other. In each, the subtle touches which lend to the narrative its vivid reality are felt only in their result, and all unknown to ourselves we are made to breathe the air, to enter as it were into the very heart of the Athens of old. In each, transported unconsciously to the every-day scenes of Athenian life, we seem to become, not eye-witnesses only, but actual participators in the action. Surely, if the true test of art is its apparent absence, then is art here found in its consummate form.

In the *Republic*, following Socrates to the home of his aged friend, we find ourselves one of the group who cluster round the good old Cephalus, listening with delight to the words of wisdom which fall from his lips. And when, as head of the family, he has left us that he may perform the evening sacrifice, — when Thrasymachus, arrogating to himself the direction of the argument, attempts by force of sheer insolence and bravado to impose his ill-considered doctrines upon his unwilling listeners, we enjoy with them the discomfiture of the intellectual bully, as at every turn he becomes more hopelessly entangled in his own admissions; and finally we exult in the triumphant overthrow of his brutal paradox, that the really wise man is the man who is "perfect in injustice."[1]

In the *Protagoras*, penetrating with Hippocrates into the very bed-chamber of Socrates, we listen to the breathless outpourings of the young enthusiast, and hear the sympathetic but restraining words of Socrates, who is no whit

[1] Republic, 348 D.

disconcerted or annoyed by this ill-timed invasion. And when, following the two friends to the hospitable mansion of Callias, that "bird of fine plumage which was plucked on all sides,"[1] we are at last admitted by the reluctant porter, we find ourselves in the presence of the most celebrated teachers of the day. But a few vivid touches, and each stands in the very flesh before us.

In the opposite portico we catch sight of the self-complacent Hippias, whose claims to universal knowledge are certain everywhere to draw around him a miniature court of admirers. At this moment, encircling the chair of state in which he is seated, they are listening with rapt attention, while with pompous fluency he expounds the questions which they propose. Hard by, in the store-closet, now converted from its former use to that of a bed-chamber, lies Prodicus, still in bed, — a self-indulgence which his weak health may serve to justify, if excuse may not be found for it in the earliness of the hour. He too has his circle of visitors, and already they are gathered around him, anxious to lose no time in beginning that "complete education in grammar and language"[2] which it is his boast to impart.

But we must not linger over these lesser luminaries. Directly in front of us, supported upon every side by a phalanx of admiring followers as with stately mien he paces the portico upon which we enter, behold the great light, Protagoras the Sophist! In his delineation of this character, with its odd blending of dignity and petulance, self-sufficiency and pliability, Plato has not allowed himself to be unduly influenced by his inveterate hatred of the so-called Sophists. Throughout the dialogue Protagoras is represented as an upright and honourable man, not unmindful of his high

[1] Aristophanes, Birds, 284–287.   [2] Cratylus, 344 B.

calling as an "educator of men."[1] Like Socrates, he believes that his mission is to teach morality; and, like him, he does not shrink from the risks inseparable from so unpopular a task. But the fulness of conviction and the intense concentration of purpose which characterise Socrates are here lacking. Nowhere is the contrast between the two men more apparent than in their respective confessions of faith, if so they may be called; the clear announcement made by Socrates of his divine mission, when, in the *Apology*, he likens himself to a gadfly sent of God,[2] as compared with the superficial and bombastic tone of the definition given by Protagoras of his own art of sophistry.[3] For the most part, however, the words of Protagoras have the ring of reason and common sense, and would often bear application to events and situations of to-day. For instance, his remarks to the effect that all citizens are self-constituted educators of the young are well calculated to awaken a sense of the responsibilities which devolve upon us all as members of the body politic; while his views on the subject of punishment, had they been understood and adopted by his own and by later ages, would have made every prison in the truest sense a reformatory.

Before we approach that familiar figure to which Plato in his dialogues so constantly assigns the leading part, let us learn what we may of the minor characters who make the essential atmosphere for the principal *dramatis personae*, and whose eager interest in the argument proclaim them to be the progenitors of those men of Athens who "spent their time in nothing else but either to tell or to hear some new thing."[4]

[1] Protagoras, 317 B. [2] Apology, 30 E. [3] Protagoras, 316 D–317 C.
[4] Acts xvii. 21.

It is noticeable that, in both dialogues, no sooner does the discussion begin in good earnest than its original promoter, Polemarchus in the *Republic*, Hippocrates in the *Protagoras*, drops into the background; not however until we have gathered, from one and the other, an impression of the gilded youth of Athens, the class to which they belong. Their mental inquisitiveness, their parrot-like repetitions of sayings the meaning of which they have never even tried to grasp, stamp them as fair representatives of the average young Athenian, — light-hearted, empty-headed, but attractive withal in their charming ingenuousness and *bonhomie*, and in their readiness to recognise and admire their intellectual superiors, even if they do not fully appreciate their worth. But as a study of individual character, Polemarchus, whose importunity brings about the discussion on justice which ultimately leads to the conception of the ideal *Republic*, yields in interest to Hippocrates, the youth whose admiration for Protagoras furnishes the occasion for the argument between the great Sophist and Socrates upon the subject of virtue. His father, Apollodorus, whose enthusiastic well-nigh fanatical admiration of Socrates had gained him the title of madman, is the same who is described in the death-scene of the *Phaedo* as "at one time laughing, at another weeping,"[1] and as finally abandoning himself to such an ecstasy of grief, that "not a man was present but was overcome by his tears and distress, save Socrates himself."[2] Something of this ardent and uncontrolled nature Hippocrates seems to have inherited. Unable to curb his impatient longing to visit the far-famed Protagoras, he bursts into the bed-chamber of Socrates, breathless with anticipation of the treasures ready to flow from out this fount of eloquence and

[1] Phaedo, 59 B. [2] Ibid., 117 D.

wisdom. Though filled with a passionate desire to obtain the much-coveted secret of leading men, he is too much overawed by the superiority of the great man to plead his own cause, and implores Socrates to speak in his behalf; while at the same time, not independent enough to brave the stigma attaching to the name of Sophist, he blushes at the bare suggestion of becoming one by profession. But, whatever may be his weakness and inconsistencies, he is always frank and open to conviction, less wedded to the opinions which he professes, because they are not his own, but are only borrowed from the minds of others and thus may be as easily set aside as they were adopted. From his apology for not having given Socrates due notice of his intended departure in pursuit of his runaway slave, we infer a close intimacy between the two friends. Their relations with each other may be fairly assumed to be those implied in the first part of the dialogue, where the attitude adopted by Hippocrates is that of listener and pupil, the position of Socrates that of teacher and adviser; although the part played by the latter upon this occasion appears to have been a mere trial of strength, a preliminary skirmish before the more serious encounter with Protagoras.

To a character so familiar to us as that of Alcibiades no introduction is needed; and yet the *rôle* assumed by him in this discussion is worthy of notice. The motive which actuated him in coming to the rescue of the argument may have been, as is asserted by Critias, pure love of a fight; but his help is none the less efficacious, whether in warding off the prosy harangues of Hippias or in bringing Protagoras to terms, while he constantly emphasises points which modesty would have forbidden Socrates to score in his own favour.

The part borne by Critias upon this occasion is but an

insignificant one. His mere presence, however, in company with his boon companion, Alcibiades, suggests the reflection that this conversation is typical of many an actual one, to which the enemies of Socrates may have alluded when, in after days, they accused him of having instilled the principles which had shaped the subsequent career of both these youths.

About our host, Callias, we know little of interest beyond what we may gather from the dialogue itself. Weak in principle and vicious in conduct, he is said to have been actuated by mere ostentatious vanity in making his house the headquarters for the philosophic lights of the day. And yet it may be true that he was not wholly without aspirations towards better things, and that it was not simply a love of notoriety, but rather the hope of passively absorbing what he would not actively strive to attain, which led him to seek the company of the so-called votaries of philosophy, a slur upon whom may possibly have been intended by Plato in representing them as ready to accept the hospitality of a man so low in repute.

The most interesting minor characters in the *Republic* are the brothers Glaucon and Adeimantus. The points of likeness and yet unlikeness between the two are most delicately handled. While we can but feel the contagion of the younger brother's eagerness and fire, the keen insight and mental poise of the graver Adeimantus claim our deeper admiration. Both are alike inspired by a whole-hearted zeal in the search for truth, and by an unwavering determination to shrink from no means of reaching it, even to the extent of making themselves for the nonce partisans of an obnoxious cause. The close and intelligent attention with which they follow the train of reasoning, and their refusal to accept what they have not understood or cannot thoroughly approve, place them in striking and agreeable contrast to many of the interlocutors in Plato's Socratic dialogues who, like Polemarchus or Hippocrates, seem incapable of forming independent opinions.

In approaching the character of Socrates himself, one question inevitably arises: how far is the portrait given us by Plato a true likeness? Another contemporaneous portrait of Socrates has come down to us, this also from the hand of a friend and disciple. Here every detail is recorded with the minute accuracy of a pre-Raphaelite painter; as a *verbatim* report of the conversations of Socrates it is invaluable: but for more than this we must not look. Although a devoted admirer of his master, a careful observer, a faithful recorder of his sayings, it could hardly be expected of Xenophon the soldier that he should enter into the innermost recesses of the great thinker's mind, or find the keynote with which every part must be brought into harmony if a complete whole is to be realised. Only a poet and a philosopher could accomplish such a task as this; and a poet Plato is in the first and fullest meaning of the word, that namely of creator. Not for a moment, in the varied aspects under which Socrates is here portrayed, do we question that absolute fidelity to truth which is the goal of all art, whether ideal or so-called realistic. The figure which stands out before us in all its marked individuality we know to be no mere invention of a dramatist, but the real, the living man. Had Plato been gifted with a less keen and delicate artistic sense, he might, as a devoted friend and disciple, have been tempted to subordinate truth of delineation to his reverence for his master, and to paint him under that aspect alone which in the *Apology*, the *Crito*, the *Phaedo*, we know and revere, — that of the hero, the martyr, the inspired thinker. Widely removed from this impression is that conveyed by many passages in the dialogues before us. Upon one occasion we find Socrates compelled to abandon a course of argument which only a mistaken conception of his adversary's ability could have led him to adopt;[1] and there are instances not a few where he takes unfair advantage of the opportunities afforded by the dialectic method to play upon the dull wits of his antagonists and mould them into whatever grotesque form his fancy may suggest. Not unfrequently a passage full of the most elevated morality and highest intellectual power is in close proximity to some childishly inconsequent reasoning or some impossible conclusion. Thus, before reaching the definition of "right living," the end for which the soul was created,[2] we are startled by the statement that "every man would choose rather to be benefited by his neighbour than to put himself out to help him";[3] while the ridiculous conclusion, artfully deduced from Polemarchus's definition of justice, that the "just man is the best thief"[4] is followed by the assertion that it is not in the nature of things for the just man to do an injury to any fellow-being.[5] And again, from the fallacious reasoning which occurs in the discussion concerning courage and confidence,[6] we pass to the beautiful description of the nature of true knowledge and its ennobling effect upon the character.[7]

It is especially in the *Protagoras* that these strange, contradictions abound. In the irrelevant sallies and flights of fancy in which Socrates indulges, in his wilful misconceptions and misleading sophistries, in the tricks which he

---

[1] Protagoras, 350 C.   [2] Republic, 353 D–E.   [3] Ibid., 347 D.
[4] Ibid., 334 A.   [5] Ibid., 335 D.   [6] Protagoras, 350 C.   [7] Ibid., 357–359.

plays upon his grave and reverend coadjutors, in his determination to get the better of every one else by fair means or foul, we are reminded of the description given later in the *Republic*[1] of very young men who, it is said, "when they first taste the sweets of argument, use it as a plaything, always employing it to contradict and to refute others, in imitation of those by whom they themselves have been refuted, and delighting like puppies in worrying and tearing in pieces (by means of argument) all those who come near them."

To account for this novel aspect of the character of Socrates and for these many apparent inequalities and inconsistencies of thought, we may suppose that he is adopting for the moment the eristic method which he elsewhere condemns, and is holding up the old processes to ridicule, thus compelling the ultimate adoption of his own method. Or we may assume that Plato wishes us to see in Socrates the inexperienced theorist, whose opinions, whose conceptions of truth even, are of secondary importance as compared with the method by which they may be reached and maintained. That Plato intended to convey this impression of extreme youth may be inferred from the passage where Socrates speaks of himself and Hippocrates as yet too young to discuss such subjects exhaustively,[2] or that in which Socrates is dismissed by Protagoras with the patronising prophecy that he will "one day take rank amongst men of note."[3] Nor is it necessary to relinquish this theory on the charge to which it is undeniably open, — that of chronological inaccuracy, — for, like many another great artist, Plato frequently makes truth of detail subservient to truth of idea. Often in some masterpiece of art representative men of every age are to be seen

[1] Republic, 539 B.   [2] Protagoras, 314 B.   [3] Ibid., 361 E.

grouped together upon one canvas; by thus sacrificing the unities of time and place, the painter is but the more faithful to the truth which it is his purpose to illustrate. And so Plato would doubtless allow no consideration of detail to interfere with his object, if he deemed that the merits of the method by which we may "test the truth and our own selves" might best be proven by demonstrating its superiority, even in its earliest stage, before it was associated with any definite views, in dealing with so formidable an adversary as Protagoras himself.

But, whatever hypothesis we adopt, we certainly derive from this delineation of Socrates the impression of a man who, in love with his own method, delights in it for its own sake, enjoying "the chase as much as the object of the chase, the journey as much as the journey's end."[1] None the less clearly, however, through all these vagaries, may be traced the salutary effects of the new system whose aim it was to force upon men the conviction that a "life without self-examination is not worth living."[2]

That the most inveterate enmity should have been excited by the course which Socrates pursued cannot be a surprise to any student of human nature. The man who makes it his life's object, not only to insist upon the necessity of self-study, but to make men actually convict themselves of culpable ignorance, can hope for no quarter at the hands of those who, though not invulnerable to the stings of the "gadfly sent of God," will not allow themselves to be goaded into a sense of shame. But not all the listeners of Socrates were of this stamp. The eager interest excited by the subjects discussed in these dialogues, the earnestness with which the most abstruse arguments are followed, testify

[1] Taine, Philosophie de l'Art en Grèce, p. 25.   [2] Apology, 38 A.

to something more than the mental curiosity and activity which characterised even the average Athenian of that day. We can but feel that here new impulses are being stirred, new ideas are being generated.

In the *Protagoras*, day has hardly dawned, and already a company of Athenians are gathered together, intent upon defining virtue and discovering whether it is possible to acquire it; while in the *Republic*, far on into the night a group may be found absorbed in the contemplation of justice and the work wrought by it upon the soul. Not to the most frivolous amongst their number does it occur to look upon any hour as ill-chosen which is devoted to topics of this nature.

Scenes such as these may no longer be witnessed in our midst; but who can mark the wide-spread interest in all subjects relating to the conduct of life, as set forth in the very novels of our day, and not admit that now no less than then these are living questions? Our novelists are but following the example of Plato, when they present to us their theories and speculations clothed in dramatic form. They differ from him only in this, that they speak through the medium of fictitious characters, he through the voices of real men. To-day the discussion of abstract themes no longer forms a natural incident of every-day life. The theoretical has given place to the practical. Only when they bear directly upon tangible interests do men who have a part to play in the world's progress pause to grapple with those problems which, in every age, have at once fascinated and baffled the human mind. At first glance, indeed, many of the Platonic discussions, from their antiquated phraseology and seemingly obsolete turn of thought, may appear to us merely as echoes from an age long past; but, upon a nearer view, the unfamiliar garb with which they are invested falls away, and behold, the doubts and perplexities and difficulties before us are our own.

Joining the group in the *Protagoras*, let us listen to their earnest questionings concerning virtue. Shall the different attributes which go to make up this most precious of possessions be likened to so many separate gems, each preserving its own identity even when grouped with others in one cluster, or, like the many faces of a crystal, are these attributes but different phases of one harmonious whole? This surely is no idle speculation, but a problem of vital import to us all. For if we recognise virtue to be indeed " one through all, a unity in multiplicity," we know also that the perfection of no single virtue can be reached if the quest of virtue as a whole is abandoned; we know that the end to be held steadily before us, the one ideal to be untiringly pursued, is virtue in its entirety. And since by ignorance alone we are blinded to this truth, so by education alone the eye of the soul is opened to the " things that are real," and we are enabled to recognise virtue as the indissoluble bond which holds together all that is good and pure and high, and to make that " choice which is best both for this life and for the next."[1]

Nor is the definition attempted in the *Republic* one of less moment. Bearing in mind the wide and deep significance of the word justice, its old-time Scriptural sense of righteousness, we see how deeply it concerns us to know the true meaning of all that this word involves. Now as then the same incomprehensible order of things surrounds us upon every side. Still is the just man laughed to scorn, and plotted against by the wicked. Still does he behold

[1] Republic, 618 E.

> "... right perfection wrongfully disgraced,
> And art made tongue-tied by authority,
> And folly, doctor-like, controlling skill,
> And captive good attending captain ill."

Now, as then, when our dark hours are upon us, filled with dismay and bitterness of soul, we are tempted to ask ourselves whether justice is not a blind superstition or idle dream, or even the unwitting accomplice of that "captain ill" which is its bitterest foe. And therefore to-day, no less than in the days of Socrates, it is good that we should listen to the triumphant refutation of that doctrine, so subversive of all morals, which affirms that might is right. Now, no less than then, do we need to be reminded that, so long as we have breath and power of utterance, it behooves us to come to the rescue of justice if we behold her evil entreated;[1] to hear the truth unswervingly maintained, that the higher and stronger nature is, by virtue of the "law that worketh for righteousness," not the tyrant over the lower and weaker, but its protector and benefactor;[2] to recognise that injustice is the greatest of all evils which the soul may harbour, while justice is her greatest good.[3]

These are the problems, old and yet ever new, which engrossed the mind and heart of Socrates and his friends, as they can never cease to engross those who, in every age, are earnestly seeking out "the way of right living, by walking in which every one of us may live his life to the best advantage."[4]

---

[1] Republic, 368 C. [2] Ibid., 342 D. [3] Ibid., 366 E. [4] Ibid., 344 E.

CONTENTS.

PROTAGORAS . . . .
THE REPUBLIC . . . .
NOTES . . . .

PROTAGORAS.

CHIEF CHARACTERS IN THE DIALOGUE.

SOCRATES.

HIPPOCRATES, *his Friend.*

ALCIBIADES,
CRITIAS, } *Young Athenians of birth.*

PROTAGORAS *of Abdera,*
HIPPIAS *of Elis,* } *Sophists.*
PRODICUS *of Ceos,*

CALLIAS, *a wealthy Athenian.*

The scene opens at daybreak in the house of Socrates at Athens, but is soon transferred to the house of Callias.

The dialogue is related by Socrates, immediately upon its close, to a friend whom he meets in the street or market-place.

PROTAGORAS

OR

THE SOPHISTS.

PROTAGORAS.

309 *Friend.* Where are you from, Socrates? But I need hardly ask, — fresh from the chase of the young Alcibiades, of course. Well, I must confess that I too, when I saw him the other day, thought him handsome still, but a handsome *man*, — for between ourselves, Socrates, a man he is now;[1] his beard is already beginning to grow.

Socrates. And what of that? Do you, then, not agree with Homer, who says that the most charming age is when the beard first appears,[2] which is now just the age of Alcibiades?

F. Well, how stand matters now? Have you just left the youth? and on what terms are you with him?

S. On excellent terms, I should say, and never better than this very day. He came to my rescue, and has been doing a great deal of talking for me; I have only just parted from him. But I must tell you an amazing thing:

although he was present, I paid no attention to him; indeed, more than once I quite forgot that he was there at all.

F. How can things have come to such a pass between you and him? Surely you cannot have lighted upon any one fairer than he, at least in this city!

S. Indeed I have,— one much fairer.

F. What do you mean? A citizen, or a stranger?

S. A stranger.

F. Where from?

S. From Abdera.[3]

F. And were you so struck with the beauty of this stranger that you thought him fairer than the son of Cleinias?

S. And must it not ever be true, my excellent friend, that the wiser appears the fairer?

F. Oh! now I see, Socrates; you have lighted upon some wise man, and you come to us fresh from him.

S. The wisest, undoubtedly, of all now living; that is if you account Protagoras the wisest.[4]

F. Why, what can you mean? Is Protagoras in town?

S. Yes, he arrived the day before yesterday.

F. I suppose, then, it is from a talk with him that you have just come?

S. Yes; and a great deal we had to say to each other.

F. Then pray tell us at once all about your conversation — at least if there is nothing to prevent you. Let my servant give you his place, and sit down here by me.

S. With all my heart; and I shall be thankful to you if you will listen.

F. And we shall be thankful to you if you will tell us about it.

S. In that case, there will be twice-told thanks. But now listen. Last night, just before daybreak, Hippocrates, the son of Apollodorus and brother of Phason,[5] began to knock very violently with his stick at my door, and no sooner was it opened than in he came with a rush, calling out in a loud voice, —

"I say, Socrates, are you awake or asleep?"

I recognised him by his voice, and said, —

"Is that you, Hippocrates? No bad news, I hope?"

"None but good," he replied.

"That is well," I said; "but what is it? and why, pray, have you come at this time of day?"

"Protagoras has arrived," he answered, as he came in and stood by my cot.

"Yes," I said, "the day before yesterday. Have you only just found this out?"

"Yes, by the gods," answered he, "only last evening." And as he spoke, feeling his way along by the bed, he sat down at my feet.

"Last evening, to be sure," he went on, "and

very late it was too, on my return from Oenoë.[6] My slave-boy, Satyrus, had run away: I had meant to tell you that I was going in pursuit of him, but something else put it out of my mind. Well, I had got back, and we had supped and were just going to bed, when my brother said to me: 'Protagoras has arrived.' At first I was for coming directly to you, but then I considered that it was altogether too far on in the night. But the very instant I had slept off the effects of my fatigue, up I got and came off here directly."

Knowing his ardent and excitable nature, I said, —

"Well, what is this to you? Surely Protagoras has not defrauded you in any way?"

"By the gods, he has though, Socrates," answered he, laughing; "for he keeps his wisdom all to himself, and does not give me any."

"By Zeus," said I, "if you offer him money, and speak him fair, he will make a wise man of you too."

"Would to Zeus and the gods," he exclaimed, "it only depended upon that! for I would not spare my own money, no, nor that of my friends either. And this is the very reason I have come to you now, to beg that you will do the talking for me. I myself am too young, and besides I have never seen Protagoras — no, nor ever heard him — for I was still a child when he staid here before. But all praise him,

Socrates, and say that he is the ablest of speakers. Why then do we not go to him at once, that we may be sure of finding him at home? He is staying, I hear, at the house of Callias the son of Hipponicus.[7] So let us be going."

"Not yet, my good fellow," I said, "for it is too early. Come, let us get up and go out into the court. We can walk up and down there and so pass the time till daybreak; then we will go. Protagoras, for the most part, spends his time indoors; so do not fear, we shall in all likelihood find him at home."

With this we got up and walked up and down in the court, and I, by way of testing the resolution of Hippocrates, began to examine and question him.

"Now, Hippocrates," I said, "since you have made up your mind to go to Protagoras and pay him a fee on your own account, I wish you would tell me what he is that you think of going to him, and what it is you expect him to make of you. Suppose you took it into your head to go to your own namesake, Hippocrates of Cos, the Asclepiad,[8] and pay him a fee on your own account, and some one were to ask you: 'Tell me, Hippocrates, what is this Hippocrates, that you intend to pay him a fee?' What would you answer?"

"I should answer that I pay him as a physician," he replied.

"And what do you expect him to make of you?"

"A physician."

"And suppose you took it into your head to go to Polycleitus the Argive, or to Pheidias the Athenian,[9] and pay them a fee on your own account, and some one were to ask you: 'What are Polycleitus and Pheidias, that you think of paying them money?' What would you answer?"

"I should answer: 'It is as sculptors that I pay them.'"

"And what do you expect them to make of you?"

"A sculptor, of course."

"Very good," I said. "Now then, we are going to Protagoras, you and I, and shall be ready to pay him money for you, our own if it be enough to serve as an inducement to him; if not, spending that of our friends as well. And suppose some one, seeing us so very eager in the matter, were to ask: 'Tell me, Socrates and Hippocrates, what is this Protagoras, that you think of paying him money?' What answer should we give? By what name do we hear Protagoras called, as we hear Pheidias called by that of sculptor, and Homer by that of poet? What name of this kind do we hear given to Protagoras?"

"As you know, Socrates," he said, "they call the man a Sophist."

"Then, it is as a Sophist that we mean to visit him, and to pay him money?"

"Most certainly."

"How then, if the person went on to ask: 'And you yourself, what is it that you expect to become by going to Protagoras?' To which he made answer with a blush, — for by this time there was daylight enough for me to see his face, —

"Evidently a Sophist, if this case is like the other."

"In the name of the gods," I exclaimed, "would you not be ashamed to figure before all Greece as a Sophist?"

"In truth, Socrates, I should, if I must needs speak my real mind."

"But perhaps, Hippocrates, you do not believe that this is the sort of teaching you will get from Protagoras, but rather that it will be like what you got from the schoolmaster, the cithara-player, or the trainer? Each of their arts you studied, not for the art itself, as if you were going to practise it, but for the general training it gave, befitting a freeman and a man of leisure."

"Most decidedly, I think," said he, "that this rather is the sort of teaching one gets from Protagoras."

"Do you know, then, what you are about to do, or are you not aware of it?" I said.

"What do you mean?"

"I mean that you are about to submit your soul to the treatment of a man who, as you say, is a Sophist; though what a Sophist is, I should be surprised if you knew. And yet if you do not know this, neither do you know to what it is that you are giving over your soul, — whether to a good thing, or to a bad."

"But I do think," he said, "that I know."

"Then tell me what you believe the Sophist to be."

"I believe," he answered, "that he is one who, as his name implies, understands all that belongs to wisdom."

"But surely we may say of painters and carpenters also, that it is they who understand all that belongs to wisdom. If however we were asked which branch of wisdom painters understand, we should probably answer: That, which has to do with the production of pictures, and so on of the rest. Now, if we were asked in which branch the Sophist is wise, what should we answer? Which branch of production does he understand?"

"What could we say of him, Socrates, but that he understands making men good speakers?"

"Very likely we should be saying what is true," said I, "but this is not enough, for our answer itself needs yet another question, namely: about what is it that the Sophist makes us good speakers? The cithara-player, without doubt, makes us speak well about the art which he understands, that is cithara-playing, does he not?"

"Yes."

"Very good. About what, then, does the Sophist make us speak well? About that which he understands, of course, does he not?"

"I suppose so."

"And what is it that the Sophist himself understands and also imparts to his disciple?"

"By Zeus," said he, "I have not another word to say about it."

313 Whereupon I exclaimed, —

"How is this! Do you know to what danger you are about to expose your soul? Surely if you were obliged to entrust your body to some one's keeping, with the risk of its being made better or worse, you would carefully consider whether or no it ought to be entrusted to him, and you would call together in council your friends and relatives, and ponder the question many days. But as to that which you set so much more store by than the body, — your soul, the thing on which depends your whole fate for weal or for woe, — in regard to this, I say, neither father nor brother nor any of your friends have you consulted whether or no it ought to be entrusted to this stranger who has only just made his appearance. You heard of his arrival, as you say, only last night; and yet, taking neither thought nor advice about him and whether you ought to entrust yourself to him or not, here you are at earliest dawn all ready to spend your own money and that of your friends as well, for all the world as if you had made up your mind beforehand that it is necessary at any cost to put yourself under Protagoras, a man whom, by your own confession, you neither know nor have ever talked with. You call him a Sophist, but what kind of a thing a Sophist may be you evidently do not know in the least, and yet to a Sophist you are about to confide yourself."

When he had heard me out he said, —

"So it seems, Socrates, according to what you say."

"And is not a Sophist, Hippocrates, a kind of merchant or pedler, who deals in the supplies which the soul lives upon? This is the sort of man he seems to me, at least."

"And what does the soul live upon, Socrates?"

"Upon knowledge, undoubtedly," I answered, "and see to it, my friend, that the Sophist, in praising what he has for sale, does not cheat us like those who deal in food for the body, — the merchant and the pedler. For they, very likely, do not know themselves which of the supplies they carry about are good or which bad for the body, but they praise alike every thing they have for sale, nor do any of those who buy from them know any better, unless by chance one of them is a professional trainer or physician. In like manner they who carry their learning about from city to city, driving a petty trade with it, and offering it for sale to any one who wishes to buy, these also praise all that they have for sale. And I imagine, my excellent friend, that some of these also do not know whether what they sell is good or bad for the soul, and they who buy of them are in the same case, unless by chance one of them is a physician of the soul. If you then happen to understand which of these things are good and which bad, you may safely buy learning of Protagoras or of any other man; but, if you do not know, then have a care, my good fellow, lest you emperil that which you hold most dear, and risk it upon 314 the hazard of a die. For surely there is much greater risk in buying knowledge than in buying food. For meat and drink when a man has bought them from the merchant he may carry home in suitable vessels, and before taking them into the body either by eating or drinking, he may stow them away in his house, and having summoned some expert consult with him as to what he should eat and drink, and what he should not, and how much and when; so that in this purchase the risk is not great. But there is no suitable vessel in which knowledge may be carried home; for when a man has paid the price he receives the knowledge into his very soul, and must go his way either injured or benefited. Let us, then, look into these matters with the help of men older than ourselves, for we are as yet rather young to discuss such a subject. But still we will go and hear the man, inasmuch as that was our original intention, and, after we have heard him we will converse with the others also. For not only is Protagoras here, but also Hippias' of Elis, and I believe Prodicus the Ceian besides,[10] and many other wise men."

Thus agreed, we set out, but, when we came to the vestibule we remained there standing; for we were in the midst of discussing some question which had come up on the way, and in order not to leave it unfinished, but to make an end of it before going in, we stood in the vestibule talking it over until we came to an understanding. Now, the porter, a eunuch, must have overheard us: and so overrun is the house with Sophists, that he, I suppose, has lost all patience with those who frequent it; for on our knocking at the door he opened it indeed, but the moment he saw us, "Pshaw, only more Sophists!" he exclaimed: "my master is busy;" and with this he clapped the door to with both hands as violently as he was able. We then began to knock again, whereupon by way of answer he called out to us through the closed door:—

"Did you not hear me say, you fellows, that he is busy?"

"But, my friend," I said, "we have not come to see Callias, nor are we Sophists, so do not be alarmed. It is Protagoras we have come to see; pray be good enough then to announce us."

Most unwillingly even then did the man open the door.

On entering, we came upon Protagoras who was walking in the portico.[11] Next to him on the one side walked Callias the son of Hipponicus, and Paralus the son of Pericles, his half-brother on the mother's side, and Charmides the son of Glaucon. And on the other side were Xanthippus the other son of Pericles, and Philippides the son of Philomelus, and Antimoerus of Mende, who is the most noted of all the disciples of Protagoras and is studying the art as a profession, to become a Sophist.[12] And of the throng who followed on behind listening to his words, the greater part were strangers whom Protagoras draws from out of the various cities through which he passes, like Orpheus bewitching them by his voice, while they follow after, by his voice bewitched. Certain of the band, however, were natives of the place. And, as I looked at this band, I was most of all delighted to see how skilfully they avoided getting into the way of Protagoras. Whenever he and they who were with him turned, these listeners, dividing in the midst, would range themselves in orderly fashion on this side and that, after which, wheeling round in a circle, they would fall behind again in capital style.

And then, as Homer says, 'uplifting mine eyes, I beheld'[13] Hippias the Eleian, seated in the opposite portico, on a chair of state; while around him upon benches were seated Eryximachus the son of Acumenus, and Phaedrus the Myrrhinusian, and Andron the son of Androtion;[14] and of the strangers present some were his own fellow-citizens, and some from other parts. They appeared to be asking Hippias questions in regard to nature and the heavenly bodies, and he, seated upon his throne, passed in review what was asked by each one, and gave judgment upon it.

And furthermore, 'on Tantalus also I looked;'[15] for you must know that Prodicus of Ceos was staying there as well. He was in a certain room which was formerly used by Hipponicus as a store-closet,[16] but which now, because of his many guests, Callias had cleared out and turned into a guest-chamber. And Prodicus was still in bed, wrapped up in skins and coverings, a great many of them, as it appeared. In one of the seats nearest him was Pausanias of the deme of Cerameis,[17] and with Pausanias a youth, a mere stripling, of mien so fair that I could but imagine his nature to be both fair and upright. I believe I heard that his name was Agathon, and I should not be surprised if he were the favourite of Pausanias. So, then, this youth was there, and both the Adeimantuses, the son of Cepis as well as the son of Leucolophides, and certain others.[18] What they were talking about, I was not able to gather from without 'where I was standing, although I was very eager to hear Prodicus, for I hold him to

316 be an exceedingly wise and an inspired man; but the deep tones of his voice made the room resound with an echo which confused all that was said.

Hardly had we entered, when, following close upon us, came Alcibiades the fair, as you call him, and rightly too I think, and with him Critias the son of Callaeschrus.[19]

On first entering the room we spent a few moments in looking about us, and then going up to Protagoras I said, —

"We have come, Protagoras, to see you, Hippocrates and I."

"Do you wish," said he, "to speak to me alone, or before these other people?"

"It makes no difference to us," I said; "but, when you have heard what has brought us here, you yourself shall decide."

"And what, may I ask, has brought you?"

"Hippocrates, whom you see here, is a native of this place, the son of Apollodorus, of a great and wealthy family, and a match, I should say, in point of natural gifts for any young man of his own age. He has, I believe, set his heart upon gaining renown in the state, and this he thinks he is most likely to do if he puts himself under you. It is for you now to consider whether you think it best to converse with us by ourselves, or before the others."

"You are right, Socrates," he said, "to use caution on my account, for, in truth, a stranger who, going into your large cities, persuades the flower of the youth to give up all connection with every other teacher, whether young or old, fellow-citizen or stranger, and to put themselves under him, that by doing this they may become better men,—a man who acts thus, I say, must needs be on his guard, for no slight jealousies and plottings and enmities of all kinds come about from this cause. Now I maintain that the art of sophistry is an ancient art, but that the men of ancient times who practised it, fearing the odium it would bring upon them, adopted a disguise behind which they screened themselves,—some using to this end poetry, as Homer and Hesiod and Simonides; some mysteries and oracles, as Orpheus and Musaeus and their school: others again have, I believe, even used the art of gymnastics, like Iccus of Tarentum and the Sophist who is second to none other of the present day, Herodicus, now of Selymbria but formerly of Megara. Your own Agathocles used music as a disguise, but was a great Sophist and so did Pythocleides the Ceian and many others.[20] All these, as I have said, made use of these arts by way of disguise, because they feared to excite enmity. But for my part I disagree with all these men, for I do not think that they by any means brought about what they wished. The leading men of the state, on whose account these disguises are used, are never blinded by them, while, as to the common people, they may be said not to use their senses at all, for they only repeat over and over again what they are told by their betters. Now for a man to attempt to run away when all the time he is so clearly in sight that he cannot possibly do it,—why, the very attempt is utter folly, and of necessity greatly enhances the ill will of his fellowmen against him, for a man who acts thus, in addition to all his other misdeeds, is accounted by them a thorough knave. I therefore take the opposite course, and confess that I am a Sophist and that I educate men; and to confess this is, to my thinking, a better precaution than to deny it. And other precautions also I duly take, so that I have never, thank God! come to any harm through confessing myself to be a Sophist. And yet many years now have I pursued the art, for the sum of my years is great; indeed, there is not one amongst you all whose father I might not be, so far as age goes. If you, then, are willing, I should be much better pleased to discourse upon these matters before all who are here present."

And I, suspecting that he wished to show off before Prodicus and Hippias and to make them aware that we had come as his admirers, said:—

"Why should we not summon both Prodicus and Hippias, and those who are with them, that they may all hear us?"

"By all means," said Protagoras.

"Shall we not then," said Callias, "make ready a place in which to hold our meeting, so that you may be seated while you are discussing?"

This proposal seemed a good one, and delighted, all of us, at the prospect of listening to learned men, we ourselves seized the benches and chairs, and arranged them near Hippias where there were a number of benches already. Meanwhile Callias and Alcibiades made Prodicus get up from the couch where he was lying, and came in bringing with them both him and all his company.

When we were all seated, Protagoras began thus:—

"Now that all these people are assembled, Socrates, I will beg you to repeat what you said to me a little while ago about this youth."

"In speaking of our reason for coming, Protagoras," I answered, "I shall begin in the same way that I did just now: Hippocrates here has set his heart upon putting himself under you, and he would be glad to know what will be the effect upon him if he does this. This is all the speech we have to make."

Then Protagoras took up the discourse, and said:—

"Young man, this is how it will be with you if you put yourself under me. The very first day you spend under my teaching you will return home a better man, and the next day it will be the same, and each succeeding day you will grow in goodness."

On hearing this I observed:—

"What you say, Protagoras, is nothing surprising, but a matter of course; for even at your age, and wise man that you are, if some one were to teach you what you happened not to know, you would be the better for it. But that was not what I meant. Suppose that the desire which Hippocrates has most at heart were on a sudden to change, and he become bent upon joining that youth who has lately come to live here,—Zeuxippus of Heracleia,[21]—and that, going to him just as he has now come to you, he were to hear from him the very same things he has just heard from you, that each day spent under his teaching he would go on improving and growing better and better; and suppose that he were to ask, 'What do you mean by saying that I shall grow better, and in what shall I improve?' Zeuxippus would answer, 'In painting.' And if he put himself under Orthagoras of Thebes,[22] and heard the same from him that he has from you, and asked in what he is to improve day by day by coming under his care, he would be told, 'In flute-playing.'

Do you then now speak in your turn and answer this youth and me who am questioning you in his name: We understand that Hippocrates here, on the very first day he puts himself under Protagoras, is to return home a better man, and on each succeeding day is to improve in like degree, — but in what way, Protagoras, and in what subject?"

When he had heard me out, Protagoras said:—
"You are an excellent questioner, Socrates, and I take pleasure in answering those who ask good questions. Well then, Hippocrates in coming to me will not undergo what he would have had to undergo in joining any other of the Sophists; for they do dishonour to the youths who, having just escaped from the arts, are led back to the arts again, and against their will plunged into the study of calculation and astronomy and geometry and music,"—as he said this he cast a significant glance at Hippias, —"but he who comes to me will learn nothing but what he came to learn,—judgment, which in domestic affairs will enable him to manage his household in the best way, and in affairs of state to acquire the greatest influence, both in speech and action."

"Wait," said I, "do I follow your meaning? I should say you were speaking of the art of politics, and promising to make men good citizens."

"This, Socrates," he answered, "is the very thing that I make a profession of."

"And a noble art you possess indeed," I said, "if you really do possess it; but I will tell you exactly what I think about this. I have never believed, Protagoras, that the art can be taught at all, and yet when you say it can I know not how to disbelieve you. I am bound, however, to declare my reason for believing that it can neither be taught, nor procured by one man for another.

That the Athenians are shrewd men is well known to me, as it is to all the other Greeks. Now I notice that whenever we come together in the assembly, and action is to be taken by the state about matters which relate to building, the builders are summoned to give their advice in regard to buildings, and in case of ship-building, then the ship-wrights are summoned; and so on of all other matters which they think may be taught and learned. And if any other man whom the people do not regard as a skilled workman undertakes to give his advice, then, be he never so well-favoured and rich and high born, they accept it none the more for that, but laugh him to scorn and hoot at him until he who is trying to speak is actually hooted down, and either stops of his own accord, or is arrested by the city guard and turned out by order of the prytanes.[23] This, then, is the action they take in regard to arts which they think may be professed; but when they come to deliberate on any thing touching the management of the state, then indeed may any man arise and give his advice, carpenter as well as blacksmith, cobbler and shipmaster, rich and poor, well born and of low degree.[24] And when these undertake to give advice no one casts in their teeth, as in the former instance, that they have never learned the art nor had any teacher in it; from which it is evident that the Athenians do not believe it can be taught.

Nor does this hold good only where the interests of the state are concerned. In private life also, even the best and wisest are not able to impart to others this virtue [25] which, as citizens, they themselves possess. There is Pericles, the father of these youths. He has educated them well and carefully in all that is to be acquired 320 from schoolmasters, but the very thing in which he most excels he neither teaches them himself, nor imparts to them through another. Like sacred cattle [26] left to range at will, they are allowed to roam about by themselves, on the mere chance that they may somewhere fall in with virtue. And perhaps you may remember, how in the case of Cleinias,[27] the younger brother of Alcibiades, this same man Pericles, who was his guardian, fearful lest he might be ruined by his brother, took him away, and sent him to Ariphron to be educated. But before six months had passed, Ariphron sent him back to his guardian, because he could do nothing with him. And I could name any number of men besides, who although good themselves, have never made any one better,— whether those of their own kin or strangers. And so, Protagoras, when I consider all these things, I come to the conclusion that virtue cannot be taught at all; but then again, when I hear you talking in this way, I am staggered, and begin to think there is something in what you say, for I hold you to be a man of varied experience, who have learned many things from others, and have found out many for yourself. If then you can bring forth any convincing proof to show us that virtue can be taught, do not, I beg of you, begrudge it to us."

"Most certainly, Socrates," said he, "I shall not begrudge it. But tell me, how would you rather have me prove my point? in a myth, as an old man does to young people, or by means of argument?"

Whereupon a number of those who were seated there, called out to him to prove it in whichever way he preferred.

"It seems to me, then," he said, "that the myth would be the most pleasing way.

Time was when gods indeed existed, but mortal race there was none. But when, as foreordained, the hour had arrived for living creatures to come into being, the gods fashioned them within the bowels of the earth from combinations of fire and water and such other elements as may be blended with these. And upon the eve of bringing them forth into the light of day, the gods appointed Prometheus and Epimetheus [28] to put the finishing touches to the work, and to dispense the divers faculties to each race as best befitted it.

Then Epimetheus begged Prometheus to let him make the distribution. 'And you,' he said, 'after it is made, shall inspect it.' Thereupon, having won the consent of Prometheus, he began his task. Now in the distribution, some he endowed not with swiftness but with strength, while to the weaker he assigned swiftness; to some he gave armour, while for the unarmed, by bestowing upon them some special physical characteristic, he contrived also a means of protection. Thus, to those whom he made small he gave wings for flying away, or else the capacity for living under ground, while their size was the safeguard of those who were large; and always in dispensing the faculties he sought to offset one by another, planning all with a view to prevent the extinction of any race. Then, having provided them with means of escape from mutual destruction, he contrived protection for them against the seasons, wrapping them around with thick hair and tough skins, suitable both for warding off the winter storms and for keeping out the summer heat, and serviceable also as a couch, that each creature might have growing upon him his own bed; and to some he gave horny hoofs to cover their feet, to others claws and stiff callous skins. After this he devised for the different races different kinds of food; for some, herbs of the earth, for some, fruits of the trees, and for others, roots; but certain of them he appointed to serve as food for other creatures. There were those again whom he made to have few offspring, while those who were constantly exposed to destruction he made to be prolific, and so provided for the continuance of the race. And in this way it happened that Epimetheus, who was not very wise, had used up all the faculties before he knew it. The race of men still remained incomplete, and he in despair knew not what to do. While he was in this strait came Prometheus to inspect the distribution, and beheld the rest of creation suitably provided with all necessities, but man still naked and helpless, having neither resting-place nor means of defence; and yet already the day appointed was at hand in which man should issue forth from earth into the light of day. Wherefore Prometheus, in great straits to find some way of safety for man, stole from Hephaestus and Athene [29] the art of mechanics, together with fire, — for without fire it would be impossible for men either to acquire or to utilize this art, — and thus he endowed mortals. In this way, then, man became possessed of the knowledge necessary to support existence, but knowledge of the art political he had none; for this Zeus kept in his own dwelling-place, and to Prometheus it was not given to penetrate within the stronghold, which is the abode of Zeus; and, moreover, the guards of Zeus were very terrible. But into the workshop where Athene and Hephaestus together delight in working, he did secretly penetrate, and stealing away from Hephaestus the art of fire and also that other art which belongs to Athene, he gave them to man. From this time forth the means of bodily subsistence were possessed by man; but Prometheus, so they say, was afterwards made to do penance for the theft.[30]

Now since man had received a share of the good things which fall to the gods, he alone of all creatures [31] held the gods in honour, and he accordingly took upon himself to set up altars and statues to them. And soon he invented the art of speech and of calling things by name; and he devised dwellings and clothing and shoes and beds and food which the earth brings forth. Now in the beginning, men, thus equipped, lived scattered about here and there, for they had no cities. And because they had altogether less strength than the wild beasts, they were constantly destroyed by them; since the mechanical arts, although supplying them with ample means of subsistence, were insufficient for waging war against wild beasts: for the art political, to which the art of war belongs, they as yet did not possess. They endeavoured, therefore, to gather themselves together in one place and to gain safety by establishing states; but being without the political art, they no sooner had come together than they began to mishandle one another; and so again they scattered, and again were exposed to destruction. And now Zeus, fearing lest our race should perish utterly, sent Hermes to introduce reverence and justice among men, to be principles of order in states, and bonds whereby men might be drawn together in all friendliness. Then Hermes inquired of Zeus in what way he should bestow justice and reverence upon men, — whether or not these gifts were to be distributed like the arts, the upshot of which distribution is as follows: one man skilled as a physician supplies the wants of many other men, and thus also do men skilled in the other professions. 'And shall I, after this fashion, bestow justice and reverence upon men, or shall I dispense them to all alike?' 'To all alike,' was the reply of Zeus, 'that all men may have a share in them. For cities could not exist if, like the arts, justice and reverence were shared by a few only amongst the citizens. And do you establish in my name this law,—that he who is incapable of feeling justice and reverence be put to death as a pestilence in the state.'"

323–328 [And hence, although the man who professes knowledge of arts which he does not follow is treated with contempt, in matters appertaining to government every man is listened to with respect, as being the possessor of those virtues with which good citizenship is synonymous. Nay, if a man does not really possess these virtues he must feign them, since were he openly to proclaim such deficiency he would be set down as a madman, or at least as unfit to dwell amongst his kind. We must not, however, fancy that the capacity for being a good citizen comes entirely by nature and does not need to be cultivated, for in that case it would be as useless and unjust to punish those who fail in this duty as to inflict punishment for some physical imperfection. Punishment is no end in itself, neither is it retaliation: a culprit is punished, not that his penalty may atone for his past misdeeds, but that it may serve as a warning both to himself and to others in the future. And if we acknowledge that punishment both prevents evil and counteracts its effects upon the soul, we at once admit that virtue can be taught.

As to the statement made by Socrates, that good men do not train their sons in this particular excellence, it is met by the answer that the whole life of every citizen, from beginning to end, is nothing if not an education in virtue; the fact that the sons of good fathers so often turn out badly only proving the truth that all men have had an equal chance to attain it. In illustration of this, we may suppose it necessary to the existence of a state that every member of it should be a good flute-player. Were this the case, each citizen would doubtless exact a high standard in this art from all his fellow-citizens; but the influences brought to bear upon each and all of them would be the same, and the son of a good flute-player would have no advantage over the son of a bad one, since the natural capacity of each and this alone would determine his proficiency. Even so each citizen in the state is self-constituted an educator of the young, from whose virtue he himself derives benefit.

It were nevertheless not undesirable, continues Protagoras, to seek some teacher who, more than other men, might be capable of promoting a yet higher standard of virtue; and here the great Sophist asserts his own pretensions by giving himself out to be such a teacher and as such, not unworthy of his hire. He lays, however, no obligation upon his disciples to pay more for their instruction than in their own opinion it is worth; if his price seems to them too high, they have but to take oath in the temple as to what they would consider fair, and with this he will be content.

Thus Protagoras, as he himself declares, has attempted, both by myth and by argument, to prove that the Athenians believe virtue capable of being taught, and that there is nothing surprising in the fact that good fathers beget bad sons, and bad fathers good sons.]

Having given us this elaborate specimen of his art, Protagoras now ceased talking; but so long had I been held under his spell, that I still continued gazing upon him as if he were about to speak further, for I was anxious to lose not a word. When I perceived, however, that he had really come to an end, with no little difficulty I gathered myself together, as it were, and looking towards Hippocrates said, —

"What gratitude, son of Apollodorus, do I owe you for having urged me to come hither! for what I have just heard from Protagoras is worth much to me indeed. Hitherto I have supposed that the way in which good men attain goodness was a thing about which no mere man might busy himself; now, however, I am convinced of the contrary. There is only one little point which is a stumbling-block to me, but doubtless Protagoras will easily explain this away, since he has already explained away so many things.

329 Were a man to converse on these subjects with any one of our public speakers, he would probably hear very much the same words, whether from Pericles or from any other of our masters of speech; but let him enquire into any particular, and like books they have neither reply to give nor question to ask in their turn. If inquiry is made about ever so trifling a detail in what they have said, then, like some great brazen bowl which when it is struck, goes booming on and on unless stopped by the touch, so do your orators, when questioned about any detail, spin out their talk to endless length. Protagoras here, on the other hand, is able not only to make long and flowing speeches, as he has just proved, but is capable when questioned of giving a concise answer, or when he himself is the questioner, of waiting till he has received his answer,—all of which things but few men are qualified to do. Now, then, Protagoras, but one little point do I need explained; if you will answer me this, I shall have all I ask for. You say that virtue may be taught, and if any man

could convince me of this, it would be you; but pray satisfy my mind in regard to this one thing which has puzzled me while you have been speaking."

[The question which Socrates wishes to have answered is whether Protagoras, in speaking as he has just done of justice, reverence, and other good qualities, regards each of these as a part which, although separate and distinct in itself, helps to make up virtue as a whole, or whether he regards each as but a different name for one and the same thing, — virtue itself.

Protagoras pronounces in favour of the former definition, and on being further questioned asserts that the several parts of virtue are related to one another, not like the separate particles of gold, each of which differs from the other only in point of size, but rather like the separate features of a face, each one of which preserves its own identity and discharges its own functions, and resembles in no respect any other feature.

Hereupon Socrates, supposing some imaginary interlocutor to be questioning them in regard to the several natures of these same parts of virtue, proceeds with the argument as follows:]

"Now if this person, going on with his questions were to ask: 'What was that you were saying a little while ago? Perhaps I did not hear you aright, but I thought you said that such was the relation of the several parts of virtue to each other that no one part was like another part'—I should answer: 'All this you did indeed hear aright, but inasmuch as you thought it was I who said it, you heard amiss:

331 for it was Protagoras here who gave these answers, I being only the questioner.' And supposing he then asked you: 'Protagoras, is he speaking the truth? Do you then maintain that no part of virtue is like another part? Is this really your meaning?' What should you answer him?"

"I should be obliged, Socrates," he said, "to acknowledge that it is."

"And what, Protagoras, should we answer him if after we had acknowledged this he went on further to say: 'Then holiness is not like any thing that is just, nor justice like any thing that is holy, but rather like a thing that is not holy. And thus holiness is of a like nature with what is not just but unjust, that is to say unholy.' What shall we answer to this? I for my part should maintain that justice is holy and holiness just, and if you would allow me, I should make the very same answer in speaking for you, and say that justice is either the same as holiness or as nearly the same as possible, and that it is most emphatically true that justice is like holiness and holiness like justice. But now consider whether you object to my making this answer, or whether you also approve of it."

"I do not feel so sure, Socrates," he said, "that justice can be granted in this off-hand way to be holy, and holiness just, for there is, it seems to me, a difference between them. But what does this matter? If you wish it, let us assume that justice is holy and holiness just."

"No indeed," I said, "it is not any 'if you so wish' or, 'if you think best' that I wish to examine, but rather yourself and myself. And when I speak of myself and yourself, it is because I believe that the argument may best be tested if the 'if' be left out of it."

332–333 [In this dilemma Protagoras states it to be his opinion that justice does indeed in a certain way resemble holiness, but only as every thing bears a certain likeness to every other thing. The vagueness of this statement is, however, counterbalanced by his subsequent admission that every thing has one opposite and one only; this leading to the conclusion that since soundness of mind and wisdom are alike opposed to folly, the two, on the theory of one opposite, must of necessity be one and the same thing.

Having gained the reluctant assent of Protagoras to this statement, Socrates now calls upon him, though as will be seen after a somewhat circuitous fashion, to define the position of justice, probably with the view of adding this quality to the list already begun of the several parts which go to make up virtue as a whole.]

"Come now, Protagoras, let us not grow weary of our search, but let us consider well what remains.

Does it seem to you that when a man commits injustice, he is of sound mind, the fact of his having committed it being proof thereof?"

"I should be ashamed to acknowledge this, Socrates," he answered, "and yet many men do say so."

"And shall I argue against them," said I, "or against you?"

"Pray argue first," he said, "if you are willing, against the former opinion, — that held by the many."

"It makes no difference to me, if you will only answer whether you hold it or not. For it is the opinion itself that I am bent upon testing, although it may very likely come about that I the questioner, and the answerer also may be put to the test as well."

At first Protagoras seemed to be standing

upon his dignity, and complained that the argument was an uninviting one; at last, however, he consented to answer.

"Come then," I said, "answer me from the very beginning. Do you believe that when men commit injustice they are of sound mind?"

"We will assume that they are," he said.

"And by sound mind you mean good judgment?"

"Yes."

"And by good judgment the power of right deliberation [32]?"

"This we will assume," he said.

"How do you mean? When good comes from committing the injustice, or harm?"

"When good comes."

"You admit then that good things do exist?"

"I do."

"And is it such things as are useful to men," I said, "that you call good?"

"Yes, by Zeus," he answered, "but even if they are not useful to men I still call them good."

Now it appeared to me that Protagoras by this time had become troubled and confused; he seemed in his answers to be putting himself on the defensive. And so, perceiving how it was with him, I began to be circumspect and gently asked:

"Do you mean, Protagoras, those things which

are merely not useful to men, or those which are not useful at all? Is it the latter that you call good?"

[Here Protagoras, glad to evade the real point in question, launches forth into a wordy harangue intended to prove that good things are in themselves neither useful nor harmful, but vary in usefulness according to their application.]

At the close of his speech all the company cried out "Well done!" I, however, said:—

"It so happens, Protagoras, that I am a forgetful man, and if any one talks to me at length, I quite lose track of the subject. Now if I happened to be slightly deaf, you would speak louder in talking to me than you do to others, and just so now, since it is with a forgetful man you are talking, you ought to cut down your answers and make them shorter, if you wish me to follow you."

"What do you mean in bidding me shorten my answers? Must I give shorter answers than are needful?"

"By no means."

"As long then as are needful?"

"Yes."

"And which ought I, think you, to do; answer

at such length as seems right to myself or to you?"

"Well," I said, "I have heard that you are able when you wish, both to speak yourself and to teach others to speak at such length upon a given subject that there seems no end to your flow of language, and then at other times you speak with such brevity upon this same subject that brevity could no farther go. If then you intend to converse with me, pray follow the second method, — that of brevity."

"Socrates," he replied, "against many men before now have I entered into a contest of words, and had I done this thing you bid me, and talked as my opponent bade me talk, I should never have shown my superiority, nor would the name of Protagoras have become known amongst the Greeks."

On this, knowing that he himself was not at all pleased with his previous answers, and that he would not of his own free will go on with the argument if he were required to answer, I thought that my part in the discussion was at an end, and so I said: —

"I assure you, Protagoras, that I have no desire to persist in carrying on this conversation against your own wish, but whenever you are willing to talk in such a way as I am able to follow, then I will talk with you. You indeed, as they say of you and as you yourself confess, are able to speak either at length or with brevity, for you are an accomplished man; I, on the contrary, am not able to talk thus at length: I only wish I were. But you who are able to do both, ought to adapt yourself to us for the sake of keeping up the conversation. As you do not, however, see fit to do this, and as I am rather pressed for time and should not be able to stay and hear you to the end of a long discourse, — for already I ought to be somewhere else, — I shall now depart; and yet from you I should not have been at all sorry to have heard even a long speech."

With this I got up to go away, but as I was in the act of rising, Callias seized my hand with his right hand, and catching hold of me with his left by this cloak of mine, said, "We will not let you off, Socrates, for if you go away our conversation will take a very different turn. I entreat you, therefore, to stay with us, for nothing in the world would delight me more than to hear you and Protagoras talking together. You really must give us all this pleasure."

By this time I was on my feet and on the point of going out, and I replied:—

"You well know, son of Hipponicus, that I have always taken delight in your fondness for philosophy, which I welcome this opportunity to praise and commend, and I should therefore be glad to give you pleasure, if what you asked were possible; but this is just as if you were begging me to keep pace with Crison the runner of Himera, in his prime, or to race with any other of the long-course or professional runners,[33] and keep pace with them. I should answer that I am far more anxious to keep up with these runners than you are to have me; but indeed I am not able. And so if you wish to see Crison and me running together in the same race, you must beg him to bring down his pace to mine, for although I am not able to run fast, he can run slowly. If therefore you have set your heart upon hearing Protagoras and me, you must beg him to answer me now as he answered at first,—in few words and keeping to the point. If he does not, what sort of a discussion can we have? To join in argument with others is, to my thinking, a very different matter from making a set speech."

"But don't you see, Socrates," he exclaimed, "that Protagoras is perfectly fair in claiming that he should be allowed to speak as he likes, and you as you like?"

Here Alcibiades broke in and said:—

"You are quite wrong there, Callias. Here Socrates confesses that long-winded speeches are not in his line and that in this respect he is outdone by Protagoras; but in regard to capacity for carrying on a discussion, and ability to sustain an argument both by talking and by listening to others, I should be surprised if he came behind any living man. If then Protagoras on his side will acknowledge that he is inferior to Socrates in argument, Socrates will be quite content; if, however, he claims superiority in this respect also, let him carry on the discussion by means of questions and answers, and not after each question make a long speech, evading the point at issue, and not troubling himself to answer, but rambling on until most of his hearers have forgotten what the argument is about; although so far as Socrates is concerned, I answer for him that he will not really forget, for all his jesting and calling himself forgetful. Let us then, every man of us, give his independent vote; mine is that the proposition of Socrates is the fairer of the two."

After Alcibiades it was, I think, Critias who spoke.

"It strikes me, Prodicus and Hippias," he said, "that Callias sides very strongly with Protagoras, while Alcibiades as usual is eager to win, no matter what the cause into which he may throw himself. But as for ourselves, it certainly does not become us to enter the lists, whether on the side of Socrates or of Protagoras, but rather to unite in entreating them both not to break off in the midst of the conversation."

As he ended, Prodicus began thus:—

"That is an admirable suggestion of yours, Critias, for they who are present at discussions such as these ought indeed to give impartial attention to both speakers, but not to heed each equally. For the two things are not the same; we must listen impartially indeed to both speakers, but not be swayed equally by each, but more by the wiser, by the more ignorant the less.

Now for my own part, Protagoras and Socrates, I think that you ought, both of you, to disagree amicably over each other's arguments, but not wrangle over them; for friends may disagree with friends in all kindness, but only enemies and opponents wrangle one with the other. Thus would our conversation be most successful, for thus would the speakers win most respect, not praise, from us the hearers; for respect comes from the hearts of the hearers and knows no guile, whereas praise in words is often given by those who speak against their real opinion, with intent to deceive. And then again we, the hearers, shall in this way receive most pleasure, not enjoyment, for pleasure consists in learning and grasping thought through the mind alone, whereas enjoyment consists in eating and in experiencing other delights through the body alone."

These words of Prodicus were favourably received by nearly all present.

After Prodicus spoke Hippias the sage.

"My friends," he said, "all of us here present, are, I hold, kinsfolk and relatives and fellow-citizens, by nature not by convention and law; for likeness of nature makes one thing akin to another, whereas law, that tyrant of men, is constantly running counter to nature and violating it. But for us who understand the nature of things, and are wisest amongst the Greeks, and as such are here met together in Greece, — yes, in this very prytaneium [34] of her wisdom, and not only in this city, but in the greatest and most honourable house which the city contains, — for us, I say, it would be shameful to do dishonour to this high honour and to dispute amongst ourselves like the meanest of men. And, therefore, Protagoras and Socrates, I advise, nay I entreat you, to give your consent to our acting the part of mediators and leading you both on to some common ground; and do not you, Socrates, on your side, insist upon this chary fashion of speech, this extreme brevity, if it be not pleasing to Protagoras, but so slacken and loosen the reins of the argument that it may come before us in a more dignified and seemly aspect; and let not Protagoras on the other hand, crowding on all sail and driving before the wind, fly into a sea of words, and so lose sight of land; but let each one keep to a middle course. So do, therefore, and let yourselves be persuaded to choose some one as manager and umpire and presiding officer, who shall see that each of you keep the right mean in his discourse."

These words found favour with the company, all of whom gave signs of approval. Callias declared that he would not let me off, and all begged that an umpire might be chosen. But I said that it would be a shame to choose an umpire for the argument.

"For," said I, "if the person so chosen were to prove inferior to ourselves, it would not be right that an inferior man should be set over those better than himself; nor if he were on an equality would it be right either, for he who is our equal will act like ourselves, so that such a choice will prove superfluous. But how if you choose one superior to ourselves? In very truth I believe it impossible for you to choose a man wiser than Protagoras here, and if he whom you choose is not really superior to him, but only declared by you to be so, you are insulting him by making choice of an umpire as for some inferior man; although so far as I am concerned, it would make no difference to me at all. But this is what I should like to do, in order that we may go on with the conversation and the discussion which you desire to hear. If Protagoras is not willing to answer he may question, and I will answer and will try in so doing to show him how I think a person ought to answer when questioned; and let him pledge his word that after I have answered all he wishes to ask, he will do the same by me. And if he does not seem disposed to make his answers to the point, you and I will together entreat him, as you have just entreated me, not to break up our conversation. And for this no special umpire is needed; you shall all be umpires together."

All approved of this plan, and Protagoras, although exceeding loth, was obliged to promise that he would begin by questioning, and that when he had had his fill of this he would take his turn at answering, and this time do so in few words.

339-347 [Protagoras at once shifts the scene from the political arena to that of poetry, the right understanding of which he asserts, is the better part of education. He demands an explanation of certain seemingly inconsistent passages in an ode of Simonides [35] relating to the subject in hand, and asks how it is that the poet after saying: "Hard it truly is for a man to become good," proceeds to disagree with the same sentiment as expressed in the words of Pittacus: [36] "Hard it is for a man to be good."

Staggered by the unexpectedness of the question, "just as if I had been struck by a first-rate boxer," to use his own words, and confused by the applause with which it is greeted by the audience, Socrates turns to Prodicus for support. "The art practised by this celebrated teacher and his well-known skill," he asserts, appealing alike to the self-love of Prodicus and to his passion for fine-drawn verbal distinctions, "are both needed to restore the credit of his fellow-countryman, Simonides, whom Protagoras threatens to make an end of. May not the seeming contradictions be accounted for by the difference in meaning between the two verbs to 'become' and to 'be'; and may not Simonides have meant to say with Hesiod, 'The gods have appointed that before virtue must go toil: for long and steep is the path leading to virtue, but the heights once reached, then that becomes easy to acquire which before was hard'[37]?"

But although Prodicus lends the weight of his "inspired wisdom" in support of this view, Protagoras scorns to accept it, declaring it to be more damaging to the credit of Simonides than is the poet's inconsistency which it attempts to explain, since he must be an ignorant man indeed who could say that the hardest of all things might ever be acquired with ease. Socrates then proffers another explanation which Prodicus, always ready to encourage any attempt at definition, finds entirely satisfactory. Simonides, he maintains, has here used the word "hard" in a sense not properly belonging to it,—that of "evil,"—just as he himself, Socrates, has often used the word "dreadful" in an improper sense, speaking, it might be, of Protagoras as being a "dreadfully" wise man. For this bad habit he has often in fact been taken to task by Protagoras, who asks how "dreadful" can be used as a term of praise, as if it were possible for anything good to be "dreadful."

As Protagoras receives this view with still greater contempt than he did the other, Socrates confesses that these so-called explanations have been ventured upon by Prodicus and himself solely with the object of drawing out the arguments of their adversary. At length it seems to dawn upon Prodicus that he too has fallen a victim to the irony of Socrates; and, needless to say, he allows this statement to pass without attempting to disavow it.

Socrates now gives what he professes to believe is the true interpretation of the ode, not omitting in the course of this, to bring in his favourite doctrine that evil is never voluntarily committed.

The Lacedaemonians, he gravely asserts, have ever been at pains to conceal their deep knowledge of philosophy, lest other nations, discovering that their real superiority lies in their wisdom, not in their physical strength, should begin to imitate them. Their short and pithy sayings, the result of the most perfect education, have been emulated by the wisest men of Greece, as is testified by the two celebrated inscriptions written in the temple of Apollo at Delphi, — "Know thyself," and "Nothing in excess."

Now of this same kind was the saying of Pittacus here quoted, — "Hard it is to be good," and so highly was this saying praised by the wise men of his time that Simonides was sure, could he refute it, of gaining a world-wide fame. He therefore composed the poem now under discussion, with the intention of proving that to become good, although hard, is still possible, but that the power to remain good belongs to the gods alone, and that Pittacus, in holding out a possibility of what it is presumption even to think of attaining, is practising deception, and this in the most important of all subjects, — the conduct of life.]

"It seems to me, Socrates," said Hippias, "that you have explained the ode admirably; but I too have not a bad interpretation of it, which, if agreeable to you, I will now set forth."

"Yes, Hippias," said Alcibiades, "some other time, but what Protagoras and Socrates have together agreed to do is now in order, — if Protagoras wishes to go on questioning, Socrates is to answer, or if he prefers answering, Socrates is to question him."

"I leave it to Protagoras," I said, "to choose whichever way is pleasantest to himself, but if he is willing, pray let us have done with odes and poems, for I should very much like, Protagoras, to get to the bottom of the subject about which I was asking at first; and this talk about poetry seems to me far too like the feasts of vulgar and boorish men, who, unable through ignorance to entertain each other at their carousals by using their own voices in conversation, hire at great expense the voice of flutes, which has no place there, and run up the price of flute-girls in order to entertain each other by means of this voice. But where men who are upright and honourable and of liberal education feast together, neither flute- nor dancing-girls nor harpers are to be seen, for these men are able to entertain one another without the help of foolish talk and childish pastimes, but simply by the use of their own voices, talking and listening by turns; and this in all courtesy even when they have taken much wine.[38] Such entertainments as these, if they be indeed composed of men such as most of us give ourselves out to be, need not the help of any alien voice, nor that of poets either, whom it is not possible to question about the meaning of their words; insomuch that of the many who quote them in support of what they themselves say, some assert that the poets meant this, others that, because they are talking about a thing which cannot be brought to the test. With such entertainments as these they will have nothing to do, but they entertain themselves in their own way, putting one another to the test by interchange of their own ideas. These rather, it seems to me, are the men whom we ought, both you and I, to imitate. Let us leave the poets aside, and ourselves originating ideas one for the other, let us test the truth and our own selves. If then you still wish to question, I hold myself ready to answer your questions, or if you prefer it, do you hold yourself ready to answer me, so that we may bring the subject to an end, in the midst of which we came to a standstill."

This I said and much more of the same kind, but still Protagoras would not say decidedly which he would do. Then Alcibiades looking at Callias, said:

"Do you think, Callias, that it is fair of Protagoras not to be willing to say decidedly whether he will answer questions or not? For my part I do not think it is. He ought either to talk himself, or else declare that he is not willing to talk, so that we may at least know his mind about it, and Socrates be free to talk with some one else, and likewise all the rest of us with any we may choose."

And Protagoras, put to shame, I thought, by

these words of Alcibiades, and also because Callias, and in fact pretty much every one there, was entreating him, reluctantly made up his mind to bear his part in the discussion, and bade me begin to question, since he was ready to answer.

"Do not imagine, Protagoras," I then observed, "that I am holding this argument with you for any other purpose than that of examining into certain difficulties which I have always felt. Homer is, I think, entirely in the right when he says:

'Let two go together, and one understands ere the other,39'

for in this sort is every man of us better provided for every work and word and thought.

But one man alone, 'even well understanding,' must needs straightway go about seeking till he find some other man to whom he may unfold his tale and by whom it may be confirmed. Just so I too am glad to speak out my mind, and to you rather than to any one else, because I believe that you of all men are best qualified for searching into all matters which a fair-minded man ought to consider, and especially those that concern virtue. For who could do this better than you who not only esteem yourself to be good and true, as do many other fair-minded men not gifted with the power to make others like themselves, but are able besides being good yourself to make others good also; and who have such faith in yourself, that whereas other men have concealed this art, you have openly proclaimed it before all the Greeks, calling yourself a Sophist and giving yourself out as a master of the art of education and of virtue, and first claiming pay in return for your teaching.

How then is it possible for us not to call you to our aid in the examination of these matters, and to question you and take counsel with you? I could not do otherwise."

350–360 [Returning now to the original question, Socrates begs Protagoras to restate his opinion in regard to the several parts of virtue.

Protagoras, although compelled by the previous agreement partially to abandon his former ground, still clings to the belief that these parts are not all alike: good sense, it is true, and wisdom and justice and holiness are pretty much one and the same thing, but courage certainly stands alone, insomuch that a man may be unjust, unholy and ignorant and yet may be courageous. But now the concession being granted that the courageous man is the confident one, he namely who is ready to face dangers shunned by others, Socrates forthwith proceeds to enquire what it is that gives confidence, and soon ascertains that from knowledge and knowledge alone is this quality derived. The diver, the horseman, the soldier, any man whose experience has taught him a knowledge of what he undertakes to perform possesses a confidence which can belong to no man who is without this knowledge. True some men there are who are confident by reason of their very ignorance, but this confidence is but of a spurious kind, and does not partake of the nature of true courage.

Now the concession granted by Protagoras,— that the confidence derived from knowledge is a predicate of courage — contradicts his previous assertion — that courage is compatible with ignorance. He has admitted that the wisest are the most confident. Since therefore, the most confident are the most courageous, wisdom and courage are proved to be one and the same thing.

Hereupon Protagoras waives the real point at issue, and calls Socrates to account for pretending that the statement which he did make,— that the courageous are confident,— is equivalent to that which was made, not by himself, but by Socrates,— that the confident are courageous. Nor does he admit that courage and wisdom, or knowledge, are proved to be identical. Confidence, it is true, is begotten of knowledge, except when like an inspiration it comes to us in a moment of excitement; but courage is a gift of nature and a result of the constant and healthy action of the vital forces, and is no more to be acquired than is natural strength of body.[40]

Unable to prove his point by a fallacy, Socrates begins an attack from another side. He asks whether, like many other men, Protagoras holds pleasant things to be bad and good things to be painful, or whether he is not willing to admit that pleasantness should be made the test of goodness; whether, in other words, he does not hold pleasure, in itself, to be always a good, the reverse being true of evil. This to Protagoras is so new a theory, that he is inclined to suspect its morality. So far, however, has he become a convert to the method of Socrates, that of his own accord he proposes to test the idea by cross-examination, promising that if pleasure and good can be proved to be one and the same thing, he will abide by the decision. But here, instead of following up the question in hand, Socrates makes an apparent digression, and requests Protagoras to give his views in regard to knowledge. Is it, in his opinion, true that if once the power to discriminate between good and evil be his, a man will do nothing save what is sanctioned by that power? To this Protagoras gives a most emphatic assent. And yet, urges Socrates, many people assert that men know good and still pursue evil, or as they call it are overcome by pleasure, and if you deny their assertion they confront you with this question: 'And if this is not being overcome by pleasure, what then do you call it'? Protagoras is disposed to treat this question with the same contempt which he has before manifested for the opinions of the "common people," but on being reminded of his promise to follow wherever Socrates may lead, he begs that the thread of the argument may be again taken up.

What then, proceeds Socrates, constitutes the evil of so-called pleasant things,—such as eating, drinking and indulging in other pleasures of the senses? Not surely the actual pleasure derived from them,—for this in itself is only a good,—but rather the sickness and the other evils which result from their over-indulgence. And what constitutes the good of so-called painful things, such as training and fighting? Evidently not the momentary pain caused by them, but the high and lasting pleasure which they yield. The standard of pleasure and pain is a right standard, but we need some principle which may enable us everywhere to recognise pleasure and pain in their relative proportions. Such a principle is found in the art of measuring: this alone teaches us that what is wrongfully called being overcome by pleasure, results simply from inability to discern good from evil, from ignorance of the true nature of pleasure.

Now applying this test to courage, we shall

find that brave men and cowards alike avoid what they regard as evil or painful, and alike face what they do not fear, the only difference being in the object of which they make choice. When a brave man, therefore, makes choice of what is commonly avoided, it is because he discerns in it a future good which more than compensates for a momentary pain.]

"For is it not evident," I said, "that men are cowardly by reason of their ignorance of what is really to be feared?"

"Most decidedly so," said Protagoras.

"And is not this the ignorance which makes cowards of them?"

He agreed.

"And do you agree that what makes cowards of them is cowardice?"

He said that he did.

"Then ignorance of what are dangers and what are not is cowardice?"

He nodded assent.

"Now surely," I said, "bravery is the opposite of cowardice?"

He said it was.

. . . .

"And consequently the knowledge of what are dangers, and what are not, being opposed to ignorance of the same, is courage?"

He no longer even nodded assent, but kept his own counsel.

"How is this, Protagoras, do you answer neither yes nor no to my question?"

"Go on and finish for yourself," he replied.

"There is only one question," I said, "which I want to ask, and that is whether you still, as at first, hold that men may be supremely ignorant, and at the same time supremely courageous?"

"You seem to be bent, Socrates," he replied, "upon my being the answerer. Well then, I will satisfy you, and say that after what we have admitted this seems to me impossible."

"I have had no other motive in asking you all these questions," I said, "than the wish to search out what the truth really is concerning things that have to do with virtue, and also in what virtue itself consists. For I know that when this point has been made clear, that other question will become quite plain in regard to which you and I have each of us spun out a long discourse, — I maintaining that virtue is not capable of being taught, you that it is. And as to the result just reached by the argument, I seem to see it stand now in human shape before us, denouncing us and laughing us to scorn; and could it speak, this is what it might say:

'You are marvellous men, O Socrates and

Protagoras! You, Socrates, who began by saying that virtue may not be taught, are now eager in support of what is directly opposed to this opinion, and are striving to show that knowledge is every thing, — both justice and good sense and courage. This certainly is the best way to prove that virtue may be taught, since were it other than knowledge, as Protagoras undertook to say was the case, it clearly could not be taught, while if on the contrary it is knowledge pure and simple, as you, Socrates, are eager to prove, it would certainly be surprising if it might not be taught.

Protagoras on the other hand, who began by taking it for granted that virtue may be taught, now seems eager to prove just the contrary, — that it is any thing rather than knowledge, in which case it would be the thing of all others least capable of being taught.'

And now, Protagoras, that I see how bewilderingly all things have been turned up-side-down, I have a great desire that all should appear in their true light, and wish that since we have gone thus far, we might proceed to the question of what virtue really is, and then return to the consideration of whether it can be taught or not; lest perchance our friend Epimetheus use his wiles to baffle us in this our quest, just as you say he neglected us in the distribution. Now in the myth, Prometheus was far more after my own heart than Epimetheus, and it is by his example that I busy myself with all these questions, and exercise forethought over my whole life; and, as I said in the beginning, with you of all men would I most gladly, if you are so minded, enter upon this search."

And Protagoras said: —

"I approve your zeal, Socrates, and the result which has been reached by the argument. I believe that in most respects I am not at all a bad man, and certainly I am the least envious of human beings. Often in speaking of you to others, I have said that of all men with whom I have had to do, certainly amongst those of your own age, I prize you by far the most highly; and I now add that I should not be surprised if you were one day to take rank, on the score of wisdom, amongst men of note. At some future time then, if you wish, we will treat all these matters at length; now, however, it is time to turn to something else."

"Well," said I, "we must so do if you think it best. Indeed, long ago I ought to have been where I said I was going, but I staid to oblige our excellent friend Callias."

Having exchanged these words, we went our ways.

THE REPUBLIC.

THESE selections are from Book I. and the first half of Book II., which form what may be called the Introduction to the Republic.

THE REPUBLIC.

CHIEF CHARACTERS IN THE DIALOGUE.

SOCRATES.

GLAUCON,
ADEIMANTUS, } *Young Athenians, sons of* ARISTON.

CEPHALUS,
POLEMARCHUS, *son of Cephalus,* } *Residents in the Peiraeus.*

THRASYMACHUS *of Chalcedon, a Rhetorician.*

CLEITOPHON, *an admirer of Thrasymachus.*

The scene opens toward nightfall in the streets of the Peiraeus, and soon changes to the house of Cephalus.

The dialogue is narrated by Socrates, on the day after it has taken place, to Timaeus, Critias, Hermocrates, and one other friend whose name is unknown.

THE REPUBLIC.

BOOK I.

327   I WENT down yesterday to the Peiraeus,[41] with Glaucon the son of Ariston,[42] to offer my prayers to the goddess,[43] and also because I wished to see how they would celebrate her festival which they were holding for the first time. The procession of our own citizens I thought very beautiful, nor did the Thracian procession seem to me at all inferior. We had offered our prayers and had our fill of gazing, and were about taking our way towards the city, when Polemarchus, the son of Cephalus,[44] catching sight of us from a distance as we were setting out for home, bade his servant run on ahead and beg us to wait for him. And the servant said, plucking my mantle from behind, —

"Polemarchus begs you to wait for him." On this I turned and enquired where his master was.

"He is coming on close behind," he answered. "Only wait a minute."

"Certainly we will wait," said Glaucon.

And shortly after Polemarchus came up, and with him Adeimantus, the brother of Glaucon, and Niceratus, the son of Nicias,[45] and several others evidently just from the procession. Polemarchus began thus:—

"You seem, Socrates," he said, "to be setting out towards the city, as if you intended to leave us."

"That is not a bad guess," I answered.

"But you see, do you not, how many we are?"

"Of course I do."

"Well, prove yourselves more than a match for us, or else remain here."

"But surely we have still one chance left,— we may persuade you that you ought to let us go."

"And could you persuade us, pray, if we would not listen to you?"

"By no means," said Glaucon.

"Well then, take it for granted that we will not listen to you."

"You do not know then," said Adeimantus, "that this evening there is to be a torchlight-race on horseback in honour of the Goddess?"

"On horseback!" I said, "that is something new. Are the riders to pass the torches one to another from hand to hand while the horses are racing,[46]— or how do you mean?"

"Just so," said Polemarchus, "and besides

this, they are to have a night festival which will be worth seeing. On rising from supper we will go to see this festival, and there we shall meet many young men of the place, with whom we can converse. So do not persist in going away, but stay with us."

"It looks," said Glaucon, "as if we should have to stay."

"If you wish it," I said, "let us do so by all means."

So we went home with Polemarchus, and there we found Lysias and Euthydemus the brothers of Polemarchus, and also Thrasymachus of Chalcedon, and Charmantides of Paeanea, and Cleitophon the son of Aristonymus.[47] And Cephalus the father of Polemarchus,[48] was at home. He struck me as being a very old man, for it was a long time since I had seen him. He was seated in a chair with a cushion, and he wore a wreath, — he happened to have been sacrificing in the court.[49] We seated ourselves near him, as there were a number of chairs placed about him in a circle. As soon as Cephalus saw me he embraced me and said : —

"You do not often, Socrates, come down to us in the Peiraeus; you really ought, though. If I, indeed, were still able to walk with ease as far as the city, there would be no need of your coming here, for we should go to you. But as it is, you must come oftener; for you know very well that the more my capacity for physical enjoyment lessens and fades away, the more does my desire for conversation and my pleasure in it increase. So do not refuse to see a great deal of these young men, and to make yourself at home with us as with friends and near of kin."

"Indeed, Cephalus," I answered, "I delight in talking with very old people; for I think we ought to enquire of them, as of men who have travelled before us on a road over which we ourselves must in all likelihood travel, whether this road is rough and steep, or smooth and easy. And from you, since you have now arrived at that period which the poets call the 'threshold of old age,'[50] I would gladly learn your opinion,—whether you regard it as a painful part of life, or what account you would give of it?"

"I will tell you, Socrates," was his reply, "what seems to me the very truth of the matter. You must know that we who are of the same age often flock together, as the old saying goes;[51] and when we have met, most of the company give themselves up to lamentations, sighing after the enjoyments of youth, and calling to mind the pleasures of love and carousals and feasts, and all the rest; and they complain bitterly, just as if they had been deprived of some very precious thing, and say that whereas they once lived in happiness, they are now not living at all. And some there are who lament over the indignities shown them at home on account of their years; and on this theme again they unite in telling over and over again the tale of the many wrongs which old age has brought upon them. But it seems to me, Socrates, that they do not lay the blame on the real cause. For if this were the cause, I too should have suffered the same evils by reason of my age, and so also would all the others who have reached the same time of life. But I have met with many a man who has not had this experience, and once, I remember particularly, I happened to be in the company of Sophocles the poet, when somebody asked him: 'How is it with you, Sophocles, in regard to love? Do you still find pleasure in the society of women?' 'Softly, man,' was his reply, 'most gladly have I escaped from love as from some furious and savage master.' I thought at the time that he had made a good answer, and none the less do I think so now. For there is no doubt that in old age there is much peace and freedom from such things, since then the passions are no longer on the stretch, but loosen their hold; and then undoubtedly does the saying of Sophocles come true,—it is a release from many and furious masters. And as to these complaints, and those also against the family, there is one only cause for them, and that is not old age, Socrates, but the character of the men themselves. If they are equable and contented, then old age itself is but a slight burden; but if not, to such men, Socrates, old age, and for that matter even youth itself, is a hard thing."

And I, delighted at hearing him talk thus, and wishing him to speak further, said by way of urging him on:—

"I imagine, Cephalus, that most people when you tell them this, will not listen to it; they suppose that you take old age easily, by virtue not of your character, but of your large possessions; for the rich, they say, have a great deal to console them."

"You are right," he said. "They do not listen to it, and what they say has something in it, though not so much as they think. For the answer still holds true which Themistocles made to the citizen of Seriphos,[52] when taunted by the assertion that his reputation was due not to himself but to his city. 'True,' was his answer, 'I should not have become famous as a Seriphian, but neither would you as an Athenian.' And the same holds good of those who are not wealthy and who take old age hard; even a reasonable man would not bear old age very easily together with poverty, but neither would an unreasonable man, though rich, be ever contented in his own mind."[53]

"Did you, Cephalus, inherit the bulk of your fortune, or did you make it yourself?"

"Do you mean how much I made myself, Socrates?" he asked. "Well, in regard to money-making, I stand midway between my grandfather and my father; for my grandfather, whose namesake I am, inherited about as much property as I now possess and doubled its value many times, while my father Lysanias reduced it to still less than what it now is. I shall be content if I can leave to my children not less, but a trifle more, than I inherited."

"I asked the question," I said, "because it seemed to me that you did not care overmuch for your money; and this is the case, for the most part, with those who have not made it themselves; while those who have, cling to it twice as fondly as do the others. For just as poets love their own poems, and fathers their own children, so those who have made their own fortune love it as their own work, besides valuing it, as the others do, for its uses. And these people are hard to get on with, because they can find nothing to praise but riches."

"What you say is quite true," he replied.

"I have no doubt of it," I said, "but tell me this, — what, to your thinking, is the greatest good that has come to you from the possession of a large fortune?"

"One," he answered, "of the reality of which I am not likely to persuade many. You know very well, Socrates, that when a man believes himself to be near death, fear and anxiety come over him in regard to matters which till now have never entered his mind. The tales told of life in the world below, setting forth how the man who has here lived sinfully must there suffer punishment, he has always laughed at before, but now his soul is tormented lest they be true; and whether owing to the weakness of old age, or from being already so much nearer to that life below, he seems to see it more distinctly. Thereupon, filled with apprehension and fear, he straightway begins to ponder and to examine whether he has ever injured any man. And he who makes discovery of many wrongs done to others in his past life, cannot sleep for fear, but is ever starting from his very dreams, as frightened children do, and lives a life of evil foreboding. But to him who is conscious of having done no wrong to others, sweet hope is ever present, and she is a good nurse of old age, according to Pindar. Beautifully, indeed, Socrates, does he describe the man who has lived a life of justice and piety when he says that

> "Hovering with tender ministrations near,
> Sweet hope shall cherish his old age;
> Mid changing plans unchanged a helmsman sage
> Is hope, through life man's restless soul to steer." 54

Marvellously true, indeed, are these words of his. This then it is, in respect to which I consider the possession of riches as of most value, not to every man indeed, but to the upright man. For if in departing hence we need have no fear lest at any time unwittingly we have lied or deceived, or lest we may be leaving behind us sacrifices unpaid to God or debts owed to man, it is the possession of riches that has in great measure brought this about. They have of course many uses besides, but weighing one against the other, I should none the less, Socrates, set the highest value upon this use of riches, at least to a man of sense."

"You speak admirably, Cephalus," I said; "but as regards justice itself, shall we say that, as you imply, it consists simply in telling the truth, and paying our debts, or is this very action sometimes just and sometimes unjust? Take some such case as this: Supposing arms had been entrusted to some one's keeping by a friend who at that time was in his right mind, but who when he asked for them back had lost his senses, surely every one would agree that they ought not to be restored, and that neither in restoring them nor in telling the exact truth to a person in that condition, would one be acting the part of a just man."

" You are right," he said.

"Then this is not the true definition of justice,—that a man must speak the truth and give back whatever has been entrusted to him."

"But indeed it is, Socrates," Polemarchus here broke in, "that is, if we are to believe Simonides.*"

"Well," said Cephalus, "I will hand over the argument to you, for it is time now that I should attend to the sacrifices."

"So then," I said, "you leave Polemarchus your heir?"

"Yes, certainly," he answered laughing, and with that he went off to the sacrifices.[55]

"Tell me then," I said, "you who have fallen heir to the argument, what is this saying of Simonides about justice, which you think so good?"

"That justice consists in restoring to every man what belongs to him," he answered. "And in saying this, it seems to me that he was right."

"It is certainly not easy," I said, "to disbelieve Simonides, for he was a wise and inspired man. And you, Polemarchus, probably understand the meaning of this saying, although I confess I do not."

332–336 [The heir to the argument soon finds his inheritance a troublesome one. It is evident

* See note 35.

that he has only repeated the maxim of Simonides from hearsay, without any attempt to grasp its meaning. On being shown that to restore to every man what belongs to him might be to do him not a good turn, but an injury, he readily admits that Simonides did not literally mean what belongs to a man, but only what befits him. This, he confidently asserts, is evil to enemies and good to friends. The maxim as thus amended is at once put to the test by Socrates after his usual fashion.

There is a fitting time for the exercise of every art or vocation. The art of the pilot, for example, finds its proper scope at sea, that of the physician in time of sickness. Now when is the art of justice [56] exercised? Not stopping to reflect that the whole field of human action is covered by justice, Polemarchus confines it to a single department and replies: "In time of war." The rejoinder then follows that just as the pilot's art is useless on land, and the physician's in time of health, so is the just man's in time of peace.

Polemarchus now aware that he has made a false step, withdraws in part his limitation, and admits that justice applies to commercial transactions as well; whereupon Socrates points out that whenever money is to be actively employed, some expert is consulted, as the horsedealer in buying a horse, or the architect in building a house, so that only in the keeping of money would justice come into play. Thus it would appear that in the use of any given thing justice is useless, and that where the thing is not to be used, and there only, it is useful.

Justice then is ascertained to be passive in its nature. Now he who can best maintain a passive or defensive attitude can also best put himself on the offensive; the man most skilful at parrying blows is also most expert at dealing blows; and in like manner, the man who is the best guardian of an army is also most apt at stealing the secrets of an enemy, — in other words the just man, since he is the best guardian, is also the best thief. This, a legitimate deduction from the definition of justice as involving the idea of harm to enemies, is the view which Homer espouses in awarding the highest praise to the maternal grandfather of Odysseus, on the ground that he "surpassed all other men in thieving and perjury." [57]

Polemarchus, confounded by this unexpected conclusion, can only reply that he no longer knows what he did mean; but although unable to prove his assertion, he reiterates that it is the part of justice to do good to friends and harm to enemies. Recognising, however, the validity of the objection made by Socrates that as just men are not always good judges of character they might choose bad men as friends and good as enemies, and thus reverse the interpretation just given of the saying of Simonides, he proposes that henceforth the terms friend and enemy shall comprise not those who only seem, but those who in reality are, good or bad.

But here comes in the real point at issue — can it ever be the part of a just man to injure any one? Polemarchus promptly meets this question with his former assertion that enemies and all bad men ought to be injured. But what effect is produced upon any animal by being injured? Is it not the loss or diminution of his best characteristics — those essential to him as an animal? And so with men. If you injure a man, you destroy or impair the best characteristics essential to him as a human being, highest amongst which is justice. Now how can it be possible that a just man should be guilty of such an act as this? As impossible as that heat should generate cold or moisture dryness, so far is it from the nature of things that the just man should do a harm to any fellow-being. Such a supposition is to be combated as contrary to the teaching of Simonides or of any other sage. Far more probably did it originate with some tyrant like Xerxes, who believed all things possible to the rich and powerful. But since this is not its true definition, how shall we define justice?]

More than once while we were talking, Thrasymachus had made desperate efforts to force himself into the discussion, but each time he had been held in check by the bystanders, who wished to hear us out. When, however, after my last words we had come to a pause, he could contain himself no longer, but gathering himself together, he came down upon us like some wild beast about to tear us in pieces. Polemarchus and I both shook with fear as he shouted out at us, —

"What do you mean, Socrates, by all this nonsense? Why are you all such simpletons as to give in thus one to the other? If you really wish to find out what justice is, do not merely ask questions, and then if you get an answer, make it your boast to refute it, for you know very well that it is easier to ask questions than to answer them; but do you yourself answer and say what you mean by justice. And take care not to tell me that it is duty, or expediency, or advantage, or gain, or interest, but tell me clearly and precisely what you do mean by it, for if you talk such nonsense as that, I will not accept it."

Now I, on hearing him speak thus, was frightened out of my wits, and trembled as I looked upon him; and I do believe that if I had not looked at him before he looked at me, I should have been struck dumb.[58] But just as he was beginning to get into a fury over the argument, I happened to catch his eye first, so that I was able to answer, and said tremblingly:—

"Do not be hard upon us, Thrasymachus, for you know very well that if we have erred in considering this question,—Polemarchus and I,—we have done so unwittingly. You surely cannot suppose that while if we were in search of money we should never consent, by yielding one to the other in the pursuit, to spoil our own chance of finding it, yet now that we are in search of justice, a thing of more value than much money, we should be foolish enough to yield one to the other, and not strive with all our might to bring it to the light of day. You cannot suppose this, my friend. The trouble is that we are incompetent; and so you ought to pity our misfortunes rather than get angry with us."

On hearing this he laughed a loud sardonic laugh.

"By Heracles!" he exclaimed, "here we have a specimen of the wonted irony[59] of Socrates, and this I knew before and predicted to these friends of ours,—that you would never be willing to give an answer yourself, but would always feign ignorance, and do any thing rather than answer if you were questioned by any one."

"You, Thrasymachus," I replied, "are a wise man. You must, therefore, be aware that if, after asking some one of what numbers the number twelve is composed, you were to add: 'But look to it, fellow, and do not tell me that twelve is composed of twice six, or of three times four, or of six times two, or of four times three; for I will not take any such nonsense as that from you,' no one, as I think you must plainly see, could undertake to answer a man who put his question in this way. And if he rejoined: 'What do you mean, Thrasymachus? That I must not give any of the answers you have mentioned? What! my dear fellow, not even if one of them happens to be the right answer? Would you have me say any thing but the truth? Or what is it you mean?' What answer would you then give him?"

"Pray go on," he said. "How like that case is to this!"

"I do not see why it is not;" I answered, "but however that may be, still if it seems so to the person questioned, do you suppose that he will be any the less likely to give what seems to him the right answer, whether we forbid him or not?"

"That means, I suppose," said he, "that this is what you are about to do, — give one of the very answers I have forbidden you to give?"

"I should not be surprised," I answered, "if after thinking the matter well over, this should seem to me best."

"But how," he said, "if I were to give you an answer on the subject of justice contrary to these, and superior to them all? What then? What punishment would you then deserve?"

"What other indeed," I answered, "but that which the ignorant person ought to suffer? He ought to learn from him who is wise. And this, in my opinion, is what I deserve to suffer."

"That is really very kind of you," he said, "but besides learning you must pay me a fee."

"I certainly will when I have the wherewithal."

"Here you have it," said Glaucon. "If it is only a question of money, Thrasymachus, say on, for we will all pay our share for Socrates."

"Of course," he said, "in order, I suppose, that Socrates may go on as usual, not answering himself, but taking up the words of some one else who has answered, and refuting them."

"And how, my good friend," I asked, "can a man answer, when he neither knows nor pretends that he knows, and is moreover forbidden, — and this by a man of no small consequence, — to say a word about his opinion, if he happens to have any? All the more then does it behoove you to speak; for you assert that you do know and have something to say. So pray do not think of refusing, but be kind enough to answer me, and not begrudge the benefit of your knowledge to Glaucon here and the others."

When I had thus spoken, Glaucon and the others begged him by no means to refuse. Now Thrasymachus was evidently longing to speak in order to get himself praised, for he made sure of having the best answer in the world; but he still pretended to be bent upon my being the answerer. At last, however, he gave way, exclaiming, —

"This then is what the wisdom of Socrates comes to! Not willing himself to impart instruction, he goes about getting it from others, and never so much as thanks them for it."

"That I learn from others, Thrasymachus," I answered, "you say with truth. But when you assert that I do not pay them back in thanks, you speak falsely, for I do pay back as much as I am able to give; but I can give nothing but praise, for money I have not. That I do, however, bestow this heartily whenever it seems to me that a man speaks well, you shall not be long, I promise you, in finding out, if you will only answer; for I am confident that you will speak admirably."

"Listen then," he said; "I declare justice to be nothing more than the interest of the stronger. But why do you not praise me? You are not willing, I see that."

"If I can only first understand what you

mean," I said, "for as yet I do not. You declare justice to be the interest of the stronger, but what, Thrasymachus, do you mean by this? You surely do not mean any thing like this for instance, that because Polydamas the athlete, is stronger than we are, and because eating beef is for his interest so far as his body is concerned, it is also for our interest who are weaker than he, and therefore for us also is just."

"That is shameful of you, Socrates," he said; "you twist my argument in whichever way you can do it most damage."

"Not at all, my good friend," I answered, "but pray tell me more plainly what it is you mean."

339-340 [Hereupon Thrasymachus unfolds the following theory. The government of a state, being that which assumes control in the state, enacts such laws as suit its own peculiar form and subserve its own interest. Thus a tyranny enacts tyrannical, and a democracy democratic laws, while by an aristocracy aristocratic laws are of course enacted; but of whatever kind the laws may be, they constitute justice, and to obey them is the duty of the subject. Justice, then, and the interest of the stronger turn out to be identical.

With the passing observation that in speaking of interest, Thrasymachus is using one of the recently forbidden terms, Socrates consents to the definition of justice as a certain kind of interest or advantage, refusing, however, to admit that it is the stronger who always reap this advantage. It is, he declares, a fact not to be disputed that rulers are capable of error, and this being the case, it follows that laws must frequently be enacted by them which prove contrary to their own interest.

Here Thrasymachus yields a ready assent, not foreseeing the coming deduction that justice, far from always being the interest, is often the direct disadvantage of the stronger. The unexpectedness of this conclusion reduces him to momentary silence, while Polemarchus exclaims with delight, 'By Zeus, Socrates, that is most true!' 'That is all very well, if we are to have you bear witness for him,' interposes Cleitophon.

'But where is the need of any witness at all? Thrasymachus himself makes the admission.'

'No,' returns Cleitophon, 'for by the interest of the stronger, he meant what the stronger believes to be for his interest.'

'That was not what he said,' Polemarchus insists.

'Never mind,' rejoins the peacemaker, Socrates, 'if Thrasymachus says it now, we will accept it.'

Thrasymachus, however, stoutly disclaims any such modification of his previous statement, and even retracts the admission he has just made as to the fallibility of rulers. Do you suppose, he says, that at the very time a man is making a mistake, he could be called 'the stronger'? Is the physician, when in the act of mistaking the case of a patient, a true physician? or the arithmetician, when he errs on a point of arithmetic, a true arithmetician? If any man makes a mistake in the exercise of his art, it is because his art has for the moment forsaken him, and he for the moment is incapable of exercising it.

And thus, as Thrasymachus triumphantly sums up his argument, the ruler who is always in the true sense of the word a ruler is incapable of making a mistake, and justice is clearly proved to consist in the furthering by the weaker of the interest of the stronger.

The next sentence refers to the complaint, made for the second time by Thrasymachus, that Socrates is always trying to fasten a libel upon him by an intentional misconception of his real meaning.]

341 "And so, Thrasymachus," said I, "you regard what I have said as a libel upon you?"

"Most certainly I do," he answered.

"You believe then that I have laid a plot to damage your argument, and that this is why I question you as I have been doing?"

"I know it perfectly well," he said, "but you shall not gain any thing by it; for in all your efforts to damage me you shall never find me off my guard, nor will you be able to get the better of me in open argument either."

"I should certainly never attempt this, my good friend," I said. "To make sure, however, that nothing of the kind takes place, pray state definitely whether when you speak of the man whose interest as the stronger it is right for the weaker to further, you mean the man who might pass for being the ruler and the stronger, or the man who is such in the strict sense of the word."

"I mean him who is a ruler in the strictest sense of the word," he answered. "Now then, do me a mischief, and libel me if you can. I will ask no mercy. But you cannot possibly do it."

"Do you think me so mad," I said, "that I would attempt to shave a lion,[60] and libel Thrasymachus?"

"You tried it, forsooth, just now," he said, "but did not make much of it."

"Enough of this," I said, "pray answer what I am going to ask."

342-344 [To the following chain of statements Thrasymachus, not suspecting at first the conclusion to which they lead, yields a ready assent:

The true physician is no mere money-maker, but a ruler, so to speak, over the human body, to supply the wants and deficiencies of which medicine was invented. Every created object, whether person or thing, being by its very nature imperfect and incomplete, is dependent upon some extraneous art or faculty to bring out its distinctive properties. Thus the eye is useless without the faculty of seeing, while for the ear, hearing is an equal necessity. An art or faculty, on the other hand, being in itself perfect and complete, needs not to seek its own interest, but only that of the object whose needs it is intended to supply. In the act of supplying those needs it fulfils its own end, and thus brings about its own perfection.

Neither of the physician nor of the pilot, both of whom consider solely the interest of those under their charge, nor of the horseman, who brings out the good qualities of the animal under his control, nor indeed of a man who rightly exercises any art, can it be said that he works in his own interest; and in like manner he who exercises the art of government, if he indeed be a ruler of men in the same way that the physician is a ruler over their bodies. will ever seek the advantage of his subjects, not his own.

Thrasymachus, ever since the real import of these illustrations dawned upon him, has responded with increasing reluctance. At this juncture he breaks loose from the logical entanglement, and assuming a tone of contemptuous bravado, tries to browbeat his adversary.

He begins by enquiring whether Socrates still has a nurse, and to the mild rejoinder that it would be better to keep to the point than to branch off into such irrelevant questions, he insolently remarks that Socrates has need of one to stop his drivelling, and to sharpen his wits into a better understanding of the well-known truth that shepherds tend their flocks not for the pleasure of the animals themselves, but for their own or their master's benefit. He then proceeds to reinforce his original statement, that justice is the interest of the stronger, by maintaining that it is always the unjust man who pushes himself into positions of authority and command. The unjust man takes advantage of the law-abiding propensity which forms a part of justice, to force his own will upon the just man, who thus becomes a mere tool in the hands of selfishness. Justice, therefore, far from benefiting those who practise it, actually works in the interest of the unjust; the just man neglects his private interests in order to work out the behests of his superior in command, while the unjust man gains success and consideration at the expense of the just.

To appreciate the full bearing of the foregoing statements, we have but to consider in what esteem is held that archetype of injustice, — the tyrant. From every quarter successful injustice receives full meed of praise and admiration, or if it is ever censured, this is only because men fear, not to commit it, but to suffer from it.]

With this, having like an attendant at the bath deluged our ears with a plenteous and unbroken stream of words, Thrasymachus had a mind to go away. The rest of the company, however, would not allow this, but compelled him to remain and make good his argument. I myself also earnestly entreated him, saying: —
"Can you have the heart, my excellent Thrasymachus, after springing such a proposition as this upon us, to go away before you have fully expounded it, or understood whether it be really true or not? Do you then regard what you are undertaking to define as a small matter, and not rather as the very way of right living, by walking in which every one of us may live his life to the best advantage?"

"I regard the matter quite differently," Thrasymachus answered.

"It would so appear," I answered. "Certainly you seem not to be at all concerned for us, nor to care whether, from our ignorance of what you profess to know, we are to lead a better or a worse life. Come, my good friend, do your best to explain yourself. There are so many of us, that you will be none the worse for doing us this kindness. I, for my part, tell you plainly that I do not agree with you, nor can I believe that injustice is more advantageous than justice, even if one has perfect liberty to exercise it and is not prevented from doing whatever one may wish. Yes, my friend, let the unjust man have full power to commit injustice, whether in secret or by open warfare, all the same you will not convince me that there is more to be gained by it than by justice; and perhaps I am not the only one here who thinks so. Convince us then, my good fellow, if you can, that we are not in the right when we place justice so far above injustice."

"And how," he said, "shall I convince you? If you are not convinced by what I have just said, what is left for me to do? Shall I drive the argument into your soul by force?"

"Not so, by Zeus," I answered. "But when you say a thing, stand by it; or if you must needs change, do so openly and do not try to cheat us."

345–347 [The above injunction is not uncalled for. The last statement of Thrasymachus contradicts his previous admission,— that all men who exercise an art seek the good of others, not their own,— and thus confounds the shepherd with the mercenary dealer, whose sole object is to make a good bargain, or with the feaster, who tends the sheep solely with a view to some future banquet.

Socrates now enquires whether, in the opinion of Thrasymachus, the true ruler finds his pleasure in ruling.

Upon receiving an eager assent, he goes on to ask why then a salary is necessary as an inducement to rule. Surely the explanation lies in the fact that no benefit accrues to the ruler from the exercise of his office. In this as in every other art, the subject, not the ruler, is benefited.

Now the result brought about by each art is peculiar to that art, and has no connection with any other. The result aimed at by the physician is to restore health, that by the pilot to ensure safety at sea. If in process of exercising his art the pilot improves in health, the art of seamanship must not on this account be confounded with that of medicine. And if the physician is paid a salary in return for his services, his own art, which seeks a totally different result, must not, simply on account of this transaction, be confounded with that of the contract-maker or the payer of salaries, which benefits him only in common with many others.

Now to induce men to accept offices of state three kinds of rewards are offered, — money, honours, or some penalty for refusing to govern.]

"What do you mean, Socrates, by this?" said Glaucon. "I know about the first two kinds of rewards, but what you mean by this penalty which you say is in some sort a reward, I do not understand."

"Is it possible," I said, "that you do not understand what the reward is which appeals to the best men, for the sake of which alone those who are most worthy hold office when they consent to do so at all? Do you not know, then, that the love of honour, and that of riches as well, is considered to be, and in reality is, a matter of reproach?"

"I do," he answered.

"This is the very reason," I said, "that neither money nor honour can arouse in good men a desire to govern. They are neither willing to receive pay for governing and get the name of hireling, nor are they willing, by secretly making profits out of their office, to get the name of thief; nor again will they consent to govern for the sake of honours, for they are not ambitious: so that it is necessary to lay some stress or penalty upon them, if they are ever to be induced to take office. And this I imagine is the reason why to enter public life voluntarily, and not rather to hold back until stress has been laid upon one, is accounted dishonourable. Now the greatest of all penalties which can be inflicted upon a man who will not himself consent to take office, is that of being governed by a man worse than himself, and it is the fear of this I think that induces honourable men to govern, whenever they do govern; and even then, they enter upon office regarding it not as a good thing, nor expecting to get pleasure from it, but rather as a thing to be accepted from necessity, and from lack of men better, or even as good as themselves, to whom the office might be entrusted. If there did anywhere exist a city of good men, then would men probably vie with each other not to govern, just as they now do to govern; for then it would be clearly seen that it is the nature of the true ruler to consider not his own interest but that of his subjects; and every one who knew this would choose to be benefited by his neighbour rather than to put himself out to benefit him." [61]

348–350 [Setting aside just here the definition of justice, Socrates proposes to take up the statement of Thrasymachus in regard to the advantages of the unjust over the just life. Instead of opposing to the tirade of Thrasymachus in defence of injustice, one equally long on the other side, he proposes to use in the discussion the more informal process of question and answer. As this proposition meets with general approval, Socrates sets about obtaining from Thrasymachus a more detailed account of his theory. He starts with the supposition that even Thrasymachus must admit justice to be a virtue and injustice to be a vice; but this is by no means granted by the champion of injustice, who exclaims: 'That is very likely, my simple-minded friend, seeing that I declare injustice to be advantageous and justice not. . . . No indeed, it is exactly the reverse.' 'What!' exclaims Socrates, 'Is justice a vice?' 'Not exactly that, but it is folly pure and simple.' 'Then do you call injustice vice?' 'Not at all. I call it prudence.' 'And do you hold unjust men to be wise and good?' 'I do, that is, all who are perfect in injustice.'

This audacious statement Socrates confesses himself at a loss to answer. Had injustice been simply proclaimed a source of profit to those by whom it is not shunned as a shameful vice, this proposition could have been met as it has often been met before. But in declaring injustice to be synonymous with wisdom and virtue, we are at the same time declaring it to be powerful and noble, and ascribing to it all the other attributes which we are wont to ascribe to justice. But although this proposition is difficult to deal with Socrates is ready to attempt the task, since Thrasymachus doubtless has the matter as much at heart as he himself has. Blurting out the rude rejoinder that it is no one's business whether he has the matter at heart or not, Thrasymachus defies his adversary to refute the proposition, and Socrates loses no time in taking up the incautious challenge. He obtains without difficulty the admission, that while just men try to gain an advantage over the unjust only and not over other just men, the unjust seek the discomfiture of just and unjust alike. He then points out that the skilful practitioner, in what profession soever, since he wishes to further the advancement of his art, tries to gain advantage, not over fellow-labourers equally skilled with himself, but over the ignorant and the unskilled; while the latter, on the other hand, look to their own interest alone, and try to defraud not only their superiors, but their fellows in ignorance.

With great reluctance Thrasymachus acknowledges the truth of these statements, from which there is but a step to the admission that while the just man is identical with the skilful and the wise practitioner, the unjust and the unskilful must be classed in one category.]

Thrasymachus admitted all this, not with readiness, however, as I am now speaking; only with the greatest difficulty were his words drawn out of him, and, it being summer-time, he sweated most amazingly. And then I saw a sight that I had never seen before — Thrasymachus blushing. And now having come to the agreement that justice was virtue and wisdom, and injustice wickedness and ignorance, —

"Let us," I said, "leave this point at rest and proceed. Besides this we said that injustice was strong; do you not remember that, Thrasymachus?"

"I remember," he said, "but I am not satisfied with what you have just said, and I myself have something to say on the subject. If I were to speak, however, I know very well that you would say I was making an harangue. Either let me, therefore, speak as much as I choose, or if you prefer to ask questions, ask them, and I will encourage you to go on by nodding and shaking my head, as we do to old women when they tell their stories."

"On no account," said I, "unless you really agree with me."

"I might as well please you," he said, "since you will not let me talk. What more can you ask?"

"Nothing at all, by Zeus," I said. "If you

are willing to do this, pray do it; I then will question you."

351-354 [Thrasymachus proves to be better than his word, for he answers, to quote the commendation of Socrates, 'most excellently well.' In the absence, therefore, of any further opposition, the following result is soon reached:

Justice must ever be the guiding principle of every society, whether state or army, band of free-booters or gang of thieves; for no society can attain strength, unless its members seek to benefit not injure one another; and thus a state under the rule of injustice is of necessity a weak state. Nor does injustice further the interests of the individual to a greater extent. If he be not at one with himself, he becomes a prey to the contending emotions which arise in his own soul, as dissensions arise in a state, and soon finds himself powerless to act, like a state in a similar condition. If such a state or such an individual be found to succeed in any enterprise, it can only be by reason of some trace or remnant of justice which prevents entire incapacity for action. And not only does injustice render a man thus inefficient in action, but it makes him also the enemy of all just men, and above all of the gods, whose friends are the just alone.

'Well, feast and make merry over your argument,' is the rejoinder of Thrasymachus. 'I am not going to gainsay you, for fear of making myself disagreeable to our friends here.' 'Go on, then,' Socrates says, 'and fill my cup to the brim, by continuing to answer me as you are now doing.' He then proceeds to consider whether the life of the just man is in reality the pleasanter and the happier because of his justice. The fact that the just man is in himself wiser and better and more able than the unjust man has been amply proved, but this other question, so intimately bearing upon the way our own lives ought to be led, is one not lightly to be passed over.

Every object, whether living or inanimate, was, we find, created in order to bring about its own peculiar end, which end is compassed only by means of some virtue peculiar to itself. Now justice is the virtue of the soul, by which it is enabled to compass the end peculiar to itself,— that of exercising not only judgment, oversight and will, but every other function which right living includes. Thus none but the just man can live rightly, and since he only who lives rightly can lead a life of happiness, and since to be happy profits a man more than to be unhappy, it follows that justice, not injustice, is profitable.

Thrasymachus, no longer attempting any show of resistance, exclaims:]

"With this, Socrates, you may regale yourself at the Bendidea.*"

"It is you I have to thank for it, Thrasymachus," I replied, "inasmuch as you have become gentle with me, and no longer treat me harshly. Nevertheless I have not feasted well, but this is my own fault, not yours. For it seems to me that I have behaved just as gluttons do who, when a new dish is brought in, snatch eagerly at it and taste of it before they have properly enjoyed what came before. So I, before discovering the thing we began by searching for, namely, the definition of justice, have abandoned the quest, and plunged into the examination of whether it was vice and ignorance, or wisdom and virtue; and afterwards, when the question came up whether or not injustice were preferable to justice, I could not prevent myself from turning to this point and dropping the other, and so I now find that I have learned nothing from our conversation. For since I do not know what justice is, I can hardly know if it be really a virtue or not, and whether he who possesses it is happy or not happy."

* See note 43.

BOOK II.

357   Now I, in saying this, thought I had got clear of the discussion, but, as it soon appeared, all that had gone before was only a preamble; for Glaucon, who in every encounter is always the boldest of men, not satisfied with the surrender of Thrasymachus, said:—

"Socrates, which do you wish, to appear to have convinced us, or to convince us in good earnest, that in every way it is better to be just than unjust?"

"If it were a question of choice," I said, "I should certainly prefer to convince you in good earnest."

"Then," said he, "you are not doing what you wish. Tell me now, do you think there is such a thing as a good which we might desire to possess, not because of the things that result from it, but because we love it for its own sake, such for instance as pure enjoyment and all pleasures which are blameless and have no after-results, but consist in the pure enjoyment derived from them at the time?"

"I think," I said, "that there is such a thing as this."

"Now then, is there any thing which we love both for its own sake and also for the sake of the things that result from it, as thought, for instance, and sight and health? We may be said to care for such things as these in both ways."

"Yes," I answered.

"And do you recognise a third kind of good which includes gymnastic training, and the treatment and care of the sick, and the art of healing, and the different ways of money-making? For these we might say involve hardship, and yet they are for our advantage; and these we might desire to possess, not for their own sake, but for the sake of the rewards or whatever else results from them."

"Yes," I said, "there is certainly this kind also. But what then?"

"Under which head," he asked, "do you place justice?"

"In my opinion," I answered, "it belongs to the highest kind, where the man who is in search of happiness should love it both for its own sake and also for its results."

"But most people," he said, "do not take this view. They think it belongs to the kind which should be cultivated indeed for the sake of what are commonly held as honours and rewards, but which in itself should be avoided on account of the hardship it involves."

"I know," said I, "that this is the view they take, and this is what Thrasymachus also had in mind when, a while ago, he was abusing justice. But I am afraid I must be very stupid, for I cannot understand this view."

"Come then," he said, "listen to what I too have to say, and see if you can agree with me. For Thrasymachus seems to me, like a snake, to have been charmed by your words far sooner than he ought; but as for me, neither the explanation of justice nor that of injustice is yet to my mind. What I long to do is to say good-bye to rewards and to every thing that grows out of rewards, and to learn in what justice and injustice each by itself consists, and what inherent power each has by its own presence in the soul. This then I will do, if you think well of it. I will renew the argument of Thrasymachus, and in the first place I will state what justice is said to be, and whence it is said to have sprung; in the second place, I will show that all who practise it do so unwillingly, regarding it as a necessity, not as a good; and in the third place, that they are justified in so doing, since the life of the unjust man is far better than that of the just, — so they say. Now you know, Socrates, that I, for my part, do not believe this at all; but my ears have been so deafened by listening to Thrasymachus and hosts of others, that I am at a loss what to think; and the opposite proposition, that justice is better than injustice, I have never heard any one maintain as I could wish; for what I wish is to hear it praised for itself alone. Now you, I believe, are the man from whom I am most likely to hear this, and so I shall do my utmost to speak in praise of the unjust life, and by so doing I shall be showing you how I wish to hear you blame injustice and praise justice. Consider, then, whether you agree to what I propose."

"I should like it of all things," I said, "for what is there about which a man of sense could prefer to speak or to hear, rather than about this?"

K

359–360 [To commit injustice, says Glaucon, in the character of its eulogist, is undoubtedly pleasant; but to suffer from it is so much the reverse, that men soon learn the expediency of coming to some agreement for mutual protection. Such, then, is the origin of justice, — it is a compromise between the state most to be desired, freedom to commit injustice with impunity, and that most to be avoided, enforced submission to wrongs without power of retaliation; and this is a compromise to which no man in his senses would submit were the case not one of necessity.

In illustration of one form of injustice, Glaucon relates the story of Gyges, the ancestor of Croesus. Gyges, a shepherd and hireling of the king of Lydia, was one day tending his flock, when a great storm arose, and an earthquake rent the ground, opening a chasm almost underneath his feet. Down this he found his way, and beheld, amidst many wonders there below, a great brazen horse, containing a dead body of more than human size, which had upon its hand a ring. This, placing it upon his own finger, Gyges took away with him, and wore at the next monthly assembly of the shepherds, when they met to take the tale of their flocks. Chancing to turn the signet of the ring towards the inside of his hand, he immediately became invisible, as to his amazement he learned, on hearing his fellow shepherds speak of him as if he were not present. He then made further trial of the ring, always with the same result. On this he contrived to get himself sent to court as bearer of the shepherds' count. No sooner had he arrived there than he began to plot with the queen, and finally, by help of the magic ring, he slew the king and reigned in his stead.

Now if a ring like this were bestowed upon a just, and another upon an unjust man, it is evident that both men would take the course prompted by self-interest; for no one is of stuff so adamantine that he would keep his hands from his neighbour's goods, had he the power of taking them without being seen; and did such a man exist, although the fear aroused by this god-like attribute might induce his fellows to praise his conduct to his face, he would be accounted by all the most despicable of fools.

Glaucon now closes his defence of injustice with the following sketch of the contrasted lives of the just and the unjust man.]

"Now in passing judgment upon the two forms of life in question, we must set up the perfection of justice, and over against it the perfection of injustice; for in this way we shall be able to judge aright, otherwise not. What then, you will ask, is this contrast which you think of setting up? Let me tell you. We will take away from the unjust man nothing that belongs to injustice, and from the just, nothing that belongs to justice; each we will make perfect for his own career. In the first place, then, let the unjust man act as all men do who are skilled in any vocation. Just as the skilful pilot or the physician recognises at once the impossibilities and the possibilities of his art, and puts his hand to some things, while others he leaves undone, and even if he does make a mistake is still able to set it right, so let the unjust man who is to have success in putting his hand to unjust deeds, keep under cover if he wishes to attain the height of injustice. The man who allows himself to be found out must be set down as nothing better than a bungler; the height of injustice being to appear just when one is not just. To the perfectly unjust man, then, must be allotted the most perfect injustice; nothing must be taken away; his greatest acts of injustice must be the very means of winning him the greatest reputation for justice. If he makes any mistake, he must have the power of setting it right again, using his gift of persuasion in case any of his evil deeds come to light, and resorting to violence where violence is called for, by dint of sheer audacity and brute strength as well as by the help of friends and money.

Having then made him out to be such a man as this, let our argument produce and place by his side the just man, the man who is single-hearted and noble, the man who, according to Aeschylus, is resolved not to seem but to be good.* Take away all seeming; for if he seem to be just, gifts and honours will accrue to him as so seeming, and then it will become uncertain whether he is just for the sake of justice itself, or for the sake of the gifts and honours. Strip him, therefore, of every thing save justice; put him in a plight which is the exact reverse of the

* See note 63.

unjust man's condition. Unjust in no respect, let him have the greatest reputation for injustice, that thus his justice may be put to the test, whether it be so firm that evil repute with all its consequences may not undermine and make an end of it. Let him continue thus steadfast unto death, seeming his whole life through to be unjust though in reality just, and when both men shall have reached the highest point, the one of justice, the other of injustice, then let judgment be passed which of the two is the happier."[62]

"Really, my dear Glaucon," I said, "you are polishing up each of these men in order to present them to judgment, as vigorously as if they were a couple of statues!"

"I do it as best I can," he answered, "and now that we have the two before us as they really are, it will be no difficult task to go on and give in detail the sort of life which is in store for each one of the two. It must needs be told; and if it sound too brutal, do not think of it, Socrates, as coming from me, but from those who laud injustice above justice. This, then, is what they will say, — that the just man, being such as I have described, will be scourged, put to torture, bound in irons, have his eyes burned out, and that finally, after he has suffered all manner of evil, he will be impaled; and then shall he know that not to be, but to seem just is what one ought to wish. And they will say that far more truly of the unjust man than of the just may the words of Aeschylus be spoken; since it is in fact the unjust man, who, pursuing such things as serve some real end and not living for a mere idea, is resolved not to appear but to be unjust,—

'Garnering from the deep-spread plough-land of his mind,
Harvests rich in wholesome wisdom's ripened fruit.[63]'

In the first place, to the man who appears to be just it is given to bear rule; then he may marry as he wishes and may give his children in marriage to whom he sees fit; or he may make contracts and have dealings with any one he chooses: and in all these transactions he reaps advantage from not letting injustice stand in the way. In entering upon any contests, whether private or public, he gets the better of his enemies and takes advantage of them, and by thus taking advantage he becomes rich, and so does good to his friends and harm to his enemies; and moreover he is able to make grand and magnificent offerings and sacrifices to the gods. And both to the gods and to any man whom he may wish to benefit, he can render services far greater than can the just man; so that he must in all probability be dearer also to the gods than is the just man. In such wise, Socrates, do they speak who say that in the sight of gods, and of men also, the life of the unjust is far better than that of the just."

Now that Glaucon had finished speaking I was intending to say something in reply, when his brother Adeimantus began thus,—

"Does it seem to you, Socrates, that enough has been said on this side of the argument?"

"Why, what else is there to say?" I answered.

"The very thing," said he, "which is best worth the saying."

"You know the proverb," I said, "'Call in a man's brother to help him.' So do you now come to your brother's rescue if he stand in need of help; although I must confess that the words he has spoken are quite sufficient to throw me, and unfit me for giving any help to the cause of justice."

"That is all nonsense," he said, "but now hear what I too have to say."

363–366 [With the object of laying more stress upon the argument of Glaucon, Adeimantus proceeds to give what he calls its converse side, — namely, the point of view taken by those who profess to be on the side of justice. All parents and instructors, he says, enjoin the practice of virtue not for its own sake, but for the sake of the very benefits pronounced by Glaucon to be the portion of the unjust man who passes for just. They sum up all the good things which the gods shower down upon generation after generation of just men; and in this they are seconded by the poets, some of whom have followed the just man's fortunes even into the world below, and have shown him to us seated at the banquets of the blest in a perpetual state of drunkenness, as if forsooth that were the best reward of virtue.

As for the unjust man, it is said that not only in the other world does he meet with the reward of his wickedness, but that while yet on earth he suffers the evils which Glaucon has described as falling to the lot of the just man who passes for unjust.

But all this talk is far from representing the commonly received belief. Even those who are loudest in their praise of justice secretly believe that injustice is in reality more profitable, and they pay honour to the wealth and power which so frequently go with it, while they despise the weak and helpless condition of the just man who lives in poverty. Indeed, the gods themselves would seem to smile upon the unjust; at least if we may trust the report of the soothsayers who go about promising to secure their favour and good will by means of certain costly propitiatory rites and ceremonies, to the non-performance of which direful penalties are attached.

What effect does all this produce upon the young? Does it not lead them to believe that since the semblance of justice is all that is needful, to this semblance alone they will turn their attention, and spare themselves the trouble of practising justice? And if it be urged that it is impossible to conceal our injustice from the gods, it may be answered that it is not certain whether there are any gods at all, and if there are, whether they take thought of men; or again, as has just been said, their displeasure may be averted by means of propitiatory gifts, and we may still enjoy the advantages of injustice without losing the favour of the higher powers.]

"Now at the bottom of all this, Socrates, is the very thing which started our discussion with you, I mean my brother's and my own, and this, my dear friend it is,—that of all those amongst us whom you name as praising justice, beginning with those heroes of old of whom traditions remain and coming down to men of our own day, not one has ever blamed injustice or praised justice, except for the glories and honours and gifts which result from them. No one has ever, either in poetry or in common speech, adequately followed up the idea of the two principles, and, dwelling upon the inherent power exerted by each of them in the soul, albeit unknown to gods and men, proved that of all evils which a soul may harbour injustice is the greatest, and that justice is the greatest good. If from the beginning all of you had proclaimed this doctrine and from our youth up had persuaded us of its truth, we should have no need to be on the watch for the misdeeds of our neighbours, for each man would stand watchman over himself, lest if he commit injustice he may be harbouring as a familiar friend the greatest of evils. Thrasymachus, and perhaps others, would very likely say all this, Socrates, and more too, in regard to justice and injustice, reversing thereby their very natures, out of mere ignorance I suppose. But for my own part, I do not care to conceal from you that it is because of my anxiety to hear you take the opposite side that I have brought every thing within my power to bear upon what I have been saying. Do not then prove by words alone that justice is better than injustice, but show what work each, and each by itself alone, effects through its presence in the soul, which proves the one to be an evil, the other a good.[64] As for seeming, let that, as Glaucon bade, be put out of the question. For if you do not strip each one of its true external attributes and invest it with spurious ones, we shall say that you are praising not justice but the semblance of it, and again that you are blaming not injustice but only the semblance of that, and that you are exhorting us to be unjust indeed, but to conceal it, and are admitting with Thrasymachus that justice is a good which belongs to another man, being the interest of the stronger, while injustice is the interest and advantage of the same man, being at the same time the disadvantage of the weaker. But now you have admitted that justice is one of those greatest goods, worthy indeed to be prized for the sake of what results from them, but even more for their own sakes, —such as sight, hearing, thought, and health, you remember, —all goods in fact which are genuinely good in their own nature and not in mere seeming. And therefore you are bound to praise justice, for the reason that it benefits him who possesses it in its very essence, just as injustice does him harm. Let others praise rewards and honours; I could bear to hear injustice thus praised and justice blamed by men who glorify honours and rewards and heap reproaches upon their opposites, but I could not bear it from you unless you yourself bade me, because your whole life through you have been intent upon this thing and this alone. Do not then prove to us by words only, that justice is better than injustice, but show what work each, and each by itself alone, effects through its presence in the soul, whether hidden or not to gods and to men, which proves the one to be a good, the other an evil."

On hearing this, I who have always admired the natural gifts of Glaucon and Adeimantus, was more than ever delighted with them, and said:—

"Sons of that man so well known to us all, well do you deserve the opening lines of the Elegiacs [65] written in your honour by the admirer of Glaucon, where in speaking of the glory you won for yourselves at the battle of Megara,[66] he calls you

> 'God-like heirs of a hero illustrious, sons of Aristo.'

I, for my part, my dear friends, think this epithet well deserved, for god-like indeed has been your behaviour if, not believing injustice to be better than justice, you are yet capable of making such a plea for it. Not for a moment do I suppose that you really do believe this. The whole bent of your character is proof positive of the contrary; although I must confess that if I judged from your own words, I could put no faith in you at all. But the greater my faith is in you, the more am I at a loss what to say. I am at my wits' end to find an answer, for I feel myself utterly incompetent. And there is reason for my feeling thus, since what I thought I had entirely proved in my talk with Thrasymachus, namely, that justice is better than injustice, you seem not to have accepted at all. But on the other hand, I must not refuse to give what answer I can; for I fear it may be an impious act for a man who happens to be present when justice is evil entreated, to yield to weariness and not come to her rescue so long as he has breath and power of utterance. And therefore, it is best for me to do all in my power to help her."

On this, Glaucon and the others besought me by all means to lend my aid and not let the discussion drop, but closely to examine what both justice and injustice really are, and where the truth lies as to their relative advantages. I then told them that in my opinion the search we were undertaking was no easy one, and called for good eyesight.

"And since we," I said, "are not clear sighted, it seems to me that we ought to make our search just as people would do who had defective eyes, and were bidden to read small letters from a distance. If one of them suddenly remembered that the same letters were elsewhere to be found written upon a larger page and in larger characters, they would deem it a godsend if they might first read the larger letters, and then examine the smaller ones, always supposing the two to be alike."

"Doubtless," said Adeimantus, "but what resemblance, Socrates, do you see between this and the search for justice?"

"I will tell you," I answered. "We speak of justice, do we not, as existing in the individual? I suppose, however, that it exists likewise in the whole state?"

"Certainly," was his reply.

"And the state is larger than the individual, is it not?"

"It is larger," he said.

"Then we may assume that justice in the larger thing would be on a larger scale, and hence more easily seen. If you therefore approve, we will first make our search for it as it exists in the state, and afterwards come to the examination of it in the individual, looking for the likeness of the larger in the image of the smaller."

"This seems to me an excellent idea of yours," he said.

"And supposing we were to picture to ourselves a state during its growth, should we not behold also the growth of justice and injustice?"

"I suppose we should."

"Then when it is once grown, is there not reason to expect that we shall more easily find what we are in search of?"

"Much reason."

"What say you, then? Shall we attempt to go through to the end? It will be no slight task, I believe; so reflect well."

"I have reflected," said Adeimantus, "pray go on."

[With this proposal to construct a state, which when described proves to be an ideal commonwealth, ends what may be termed the Prelude of the "Republic." The keynote has been struck which, through the ensuing and constantly changing modulations, ever and anon makes itself heard, until in the story of Er the Armenian and the revelation made to him of the future life, we are again brought back to the original theme, and find full satisfaction in the truth that for every man, "whether he be dead or yet alive, justice is the better choice."]

NOTES.

NOTES ON THE PROTAGORAS.

NOTE 1, p. 3.

EVERY Athenian youth at the age of eighteen was enrolled upon the list of citizens, and admitted to the rights and duties of manhood.

NOTE 2, p. 3.

This passage occurs in the description of Hermes, when he meets Odysseus and gives him the charmed herb "moly" as a protection from the wiles of Circe: —

> "But while through the glorious woodland I wended my way,
> Ere I reached the wide dwelling of Circe, in simples well versed,
> As I took my way thither, a wand in his hand, made of gold,
> There encountered me Hermes: a stripling with beard of first growth
> Even such did he seem, for a youth with most charm then is graced."
> — *Odyssey*, x., 275 ff.

By this allusion to the youth of Alcibiades, Plato seems to suggest that the dialogue took place in the year 433 B.C., when Alcibiades was eighteen years old. But no date can be assigned which does not involve grave chronological inaccuracies, since it is impossible that all the characters should have appeared together at the respective ages here ascribed to them.

NOTE 3, p. 4.

ABDERA was a Greek colony in Thrace, which, although the birthplace of the philosophers Protagoras, Democritus, and Leucippus, of the historian Hecataeus, and of other noted men, was proverbial for the dulness of its inhabitants. Thus

Cicero, in one of his letters, characterises a foolish proposition which he has rejected, as "worthy of Abdera."—*Ad Att.* vii. vii.

NOTE 4, p. 4.

PROTAGORAS is said to have begun life as a porter. By assiduous study, however, he made up for the deficiencies of his earlier years, and came to be esteemed the most learned of his contemporaries, who nicknamed him "Wisdom." His celebrated doctrine,—"Man is the measure of all things; of things that are, that they exist, and of things that are not, that they do not exist," is explained by Plato (*Theætetus*, 161 C) as meaning that all knowledge is derived through the senses only. Unlike many of his contemporaries, he looked upon his duties as a teacher in an earnest light, and was fearless in the expression of his opinions (see *Protagoras*, 316 E–317 B). He did not hesitate to declare:—"Concerning the gods, whether they are or are not, I know nothing: the shortness of life, the difficulty of the subject, and many other things render such knowledge impossible;" and this bold assertion, it is said, led to his arraignment as an atheist, when without awaiting the result of the trial he fled to Sicily, and was, so the story runs, drowned on the passage, at the age of seventy.

Protagoras was the first philosopher who took pay for his instruction, his fee amounting in some cases to one hundred *minæ* (more than eighteen hundred dollars). His example was followed by his contemporaries; and on this account they were censured by Socrates as "barterers of their manhood, through the necessity under which they lay themselves to hold discourse at the will of any from whom they receive pay."—XEN. *Mem.* I. ii. 6.

NOTE 5, p. 5.

Of the subsequent career of HIPPOCRATES nothing is known, nor do we find his brother PHASON elsewhere mentioned. Their father Apollodorus, well known as an ardent admirer of Socrates, is mentioned in the *Apology* (38 B) as one of the four who offered security for the fine proposed by Socrates for himself, and is described in the death-scene of the *Phædo* (117 D) as giving way to the most passionate grief.

NOTE 6, p. 5.

OENOË was situated on the border of Bœotia, which frontier, as nearest to Athens, the slave would naturally have attempted to reach.

NOTE 7, p. 7.

CALLIAS belonged to an ancient and honoured family, in which the office of herald at the Eleusinian mysteries was hereditary. To this office, in the particular branch of the family to which Callias belonged, was added that of torch-bearer in the same mysteries, as well as that of Spartan proxenus at Athens, — an office roughly corresponding to our consul. Members of the family of Callias, moreover, had not unfrequently been sent upon embassies to the neighbouring states; and probably for this reason rather than from any merit of his own Callias was three times chosen to head a delegation to Sparta. His passion for surrounding himself with all the celebrities of the day was doubtless one cause of his rapid dissipation of the large fortune left him by his frugal father; for, as we learn in the *Apology* (20.A), "he spent more money upon the Sophists than all other men put together."

NOTE 8, p. 7.

The celebrated physician HIPPOCRATES of Cos belonged to the Asclepiadæ, a family in which the practice of medicine was hereditary, and which boasted descent from Asclepios, the god of medicine, the Roman Aesculapius. As a reward for having delivered Athens from a pestilence he was presented with a golden crown and admitted to the rights of citizenship. So wide became his renown that he was bidden to the Court of Persia, by Artaxerxes: he refused however to obey the summons, on the plea that he owed his services to his own country, and not to any foreign land.

Note 9, p. 8.

POLYCLEITUS was particularly celebrated for his figures of athletes, and is ranked in Xenophon's *Memorabilia* (I. iv.3) as highest among sculptors, as Homer is among epic poets, and Sophocles among dramatists.

PHEIDIAS was entrusted by Pericles with the charge of beautifying the public buildings of Athens, and the cessation of this work was not the least of the evils consequent upon Pericles' loss of favour with the people. Failing to convict Pheidias upon the ground of having misappropriated public moneys, his enemies finally succeeded in having him banished from Athens on the charge of impiety, because he had presumed to carve his own likeness and that of Pericles upon the shield of Athene, a colossal statue made by him, to adorn the Parthenon. Pheidias then took up his abode at Elis, where his first work was a statue of Olympian Zeus. This he vowed should surpass the Athene in beauty; and so well did he keep his promise that in token of their gratitude, so Pausanias tells us, the people of Elis appointed his family to be perpetual guardians of the statue. From the allusion here made to Pheidias, we may presume that at this time he was still alive.

Note 10, p. 14.

Like many of the other Sophists, HIPPIAS travelled throughout Greece, where he taught and lectured with a view to acquiring fortune as well as fame. He was wont to maintain that virtue consisted in being independent in all things, and he asserted his own claim to its possession, by pretending to universal knowledge. At one of the Olympian festivals he boasted that he was master of every art, mechanical as well as liberal, stating in proof of this, that every article he wore was the work of his own hands (*Hippias Minor*, 368 B-C). He was noted for his memory, and it is said could remember fifty names after hearing them once repeated. The authenticity of the two Platonic dialogues which bear his name is disputed, but the same traits of superficiality and self-importance which characterise the Hippias of the *Protagoras* are there displayed: witness the passage where he excuses himself for not coming oftener to Athens, on the plea that "When Elis has business to negotiate with any of the cities, I am always the one chosen from among her citizens to be chief ambassador; for it is held that I am the one best fitted to be judge and envoy in such negotiations as are customary between one city and another." — *Hippias Major*, 281 A.

PRODICUS made his first appearance in Athens at the head of an embassy. In this capacity he displayed such powers of oratory that he excited great admiration among the Athenians, and, finding himself much in request, remained and taught in their midst, enjoying the friendship of the most distinguished men of the day. In such high esteem were his lectures held, that Xenophon, when in prison, is said to have obtained bail for the express purpose of hearing one of them; and "Wiser than Prodicus" became a proverb to express the unattainable. His strong point was the use of synonymes, — a study which was a matter of mere guess-work, when etymology as then was yet in its infancy: hence his speculations in the *Protagoras* are not unnaturally turned into ridicule by Socrates, who speaks, however, of having attended his single-drachma reading, referring to the fifty-drachma lecture, which professed to be a "complete education in grammar and language," as beyond his means. — [Plato, *Cratylus*, 384 B.] The allusion to his voice, the "deep tones" of which awakened an echo in the room, may be intended as a reflection upon the well-known harshness of its quality; while in the description given of him as still in bed, and wrapped in many coverings, we may see a reference to his weak state of health. What we know of Prodicus inclines us to believe that, if not the wisest, he was the best of the Sophists. The summary of his excellent fable of the *Choice of Heracles*, to be found in Xenophon's *Memorabilia* (II. i. 21), is all that has come down to us of his writings.

Note 11, p. 15.

The house of a well-to-do Athenian like Callias was divided into the men's quarters (*andronitis*), where is laid the scene of the *Protagoras*, and those devoted to the women (*gunaikonitis*), the two being separated by a strongly bolted door. Each of these divisions was composed of various apartments, all opening upon an uncovered court surrounded by arcades, which, upon the side nearest the entrance, and perhaps also upon that opposite to it, formed a species of portico.

Note 12, p. 15.

XANTHIPPUS and PARALUS bore, during their short lives, the unenviable nickname of "Boobies." They were half-brothers of Callias, he being the son of their mother by her former marriage with Hipponicus.

CHARMIDES, upon the death of his father Glaucon, became the ward of his cousin Critias. That Charmides was most carefully educated is a point to be remembered in favour of his much condemned guardian. He is represented by Plato, whose uncle he was, and also by Xenophon, as equally charming in appearance and in disposition, and is said to have been something of a poet withal. In the *Memorabilia* (III. vi. 2) a conversation between him and Socrates is recorded, in which the latter asks Charmides, who has pleaded bashfulness as an excuse for not entering public life, whether a man endowed with such capacity for playing a useful part there has the right to withhold his services from the state. These exhortations seem to have been unfortunate in their effect. Charmides afterwards became one of the board of Ten in the Peiræus, appointed during the bloodthirsty rule of the Thirty Tyrants, and fell by the side of Critias in the encounter with Thrasybulus and the returning democrats.

Nothing is known of the other two personages here introduced.

Note 13, p. 16.

"Uplifting mine eyes I beheld mighty Heracles next,
His image, I say; for himself midst the gods that are deathless
Takes joyance and feasts."

— *Odyssey*, xi., 601–603.

Note 14, p. 16.

ERYXIMACHUS, like his father Acumenus, was a learned and respected physician, as well as a natural philosopher.

For PHAEDRUS Plato had a peculiar fondness, as is shown in the dialogue which bears this name. Although we are told that he was a great reader and lover of literature, nothing is known of the writings of Phaedrus. He seems to have attached value to the medical advice of Acumenus, the father of Eryximachus his intimate friend, as we gather from the opening of the dialogue just mentioned (227 A), where Socrates falls in with him as he is on his way to take a walk outside the wall, because Acumenus has advised his exercising in the country.

Of ANDRON no mention is elsewhere found.

Note 15, p. 16.

"And Tantalus, too, I descried, by fierce torments possessed,
Who stood amidst waters uplifting, that reached to his chin, —
Stood panting with thirst; yet vainly to quench it he sought:
For eager to drink, whene'er the old man bent him down,
So often the water would vanish and sink, round his feet
The black earth appear; for a god made it dry."

— *Odyssey*, xi., 582–88.

Note 16, p. 16.

In order to protect the household supplies from thieving slaves, it was customary to connect all the store-rooms with the women's apartments; but the thrifty Hipponicus seems to have required extra room to hold his stores, and thus to have reserved for them an additional place in the men's quarters.

Note 17, p. 16.

Attica was subdivided into demes, which corresponded roughly to our townships, or to the *wards* of our cities.

NOTE 18, p. 17.

PAUSANIAS is chiefly known as having been the lifelong friend of the "fair Agathon."

AGATHON'S reputation for extreme beauty is said to have rendered him somewhat vain and foppish. He afterwards attained distinction as a writer of tragedies, certain fragments from which are preserved by Aristotle. He aimed chiefly at novelty, adorning his works with the figures and embellishments then in vogue, and was ranked as the best of the second-rate tragic poets. It was upon the occasion of receiving a prize for his first tragedy, that he gave the banquet, the conversation at which forms the subject of Plato's *Symposium*.

Of ADEIMANTUS the son of Cepis nothing is known, but the other ADEIMANTUS is supposed to be the same who was implicated with Alcibiades in the profanation of the mysteries. . He was one of the oligarchical faction, and was accounted by Aristophanes one of the most dangerous men in Athens. In the Peloponnesian war he proved himself a successful strategist. Taken prisoner after the disaster of Aegospotami, he alone of all the Athenians was set at liberty by Lysander,—in reward for an act of treachery.

NOTE 19, p. 18.

In the charming youth described in Plato's dialogues, as well as in the *Memorabilia* of Xenophon, we fail to recognise the future traitor ALCIBIADES; nor is it less difficult to trace in his friend, the devotee of philosophy and literature, any likeness to the merciless CRITIAS, so soon to become the most hated of men. The accusation brought against Socrates as a corrupter of youth was partially founded upon the fact that both these men had been his disciples. The charge is disproved by Xenophon, who insists that as long as they remained with Socrates both practised self-control, because he had taught them to believe that this was right. We are told, however, that as soon as they imagined themselves to have acquired that mental superiority over the rulers in the state which it had been their object to attain, they no longer went with Socrates; for they were "by nature the most ambitious of all the Athenians, and their desire was that every thing should be brought about through them, and they themselves become the most noted of men." "It is my belief," continues Xenophon, "that had a god given them the choice, whether they would prefer to live their whole life through as they saw Socrates live or to die, that they would have chosen rather to die." — XEN. *Mem.* I. ii. 14-18.

NOTE 20, p. 19.

Protagoras asserts that the ethical side of philosophy — the task of "educating men" — constitutes the art of sophistry, and attempts to prove that former teachers of morality had escaped unpopularity only by professing openly some other art, which served as a disguise. As to the illustrations he uses, and how convincing they may have been, our scanty knowledge concerning them forbids us to form any judgment.

HOMER often, it is true, especially in the *Odyssey*, taking advantage of the rapt attention lént by his auditors to his vivid narrative, inculcates the performance of certain moral duties; while HESIOD also, in his *Works and Days*, enforces the observance of the rules of right living. But what has come down to us of the poems of ORPHEUS and MUSAEUS is of too fragmentary a nature and of too doubtful authenticity to enable us to decide whether or not the mystic teachings of these legendary poets were symbolic of practical truths and precepts.

It was probably because ICCUS of Tarentum was a reputed follower of the Pythagorean school that he is given a place upon this list. A victor in the Olympic games, he gained the reputation — perhaps the one most coveted by the Greeks — of being the best gymnast of his time. He taught that gymnastic training induced temperance, which virtue he himself practised to such an extent that the "dinner of Iccus" became a proverbial saying.

No trace can be discovered of the ethical teachings of

HERODICUS. He is chiefly known as the instructor of the celebrated Hippocrates in the art of medicine. Himself in delicate health, his whole attention was devoted to the hygienic side of gymnastics; namely, the systematic observance of the rules of health and the regimen and care of the body. Plato throws ridicule upon him for having originated the "present fashion of cultivating diseases," and declares that although by the help of science he arrived at old age, the struggle against death was nothing but a process of torture (*Republic*, 406 A–B).

Of AGATHOCLES we only know that he was the teacher of the celebrated musician Damon. PYTHOCLEIDES, as well as this same Damon, was supposed to have used the art he professed, merely as a screen for the political instruction which he wished to disseminate.

NOTE 21, p. 21.

The celebrated painter ZEUXIPPUS is more generally known as Zeuxis, an abbreviation of the longer name.

NOTE 22, p. 22.

The Thebans were regarded as the best flute-players in Greece.

NOTE 23, p. 24.

Under the name of PRYTANES, the ten groups, each of fifty senators, representing severally the ten Athenian tribes in the senate of five hundred at Athens, took turns in presiding over the senate, and assuming general direction of affairs.

NOTE 24, p. 24.

The following passage from the *Memorabilia* is a caricature of the popular notion so distasteful to Socrates, that ignorance of statesmanship need be no bar to success in public life. After giving a parody of the maiden speech in the popular assembly, which was to be expected from a certain Euthydemus, a youth wise in his own conceit, and anxious to avoid the reputation of having "learned any thing from anybody," Socrates imagines this same youth to have turned physician, and to be applying the self-same principles to his new art after the following fashion:—" Never, men of Athens," he boasts, "have I learned the art of medicine from any man, nor have I sought to have any of the physicians as my teacher; for, my whole life through, I have been on my guard, not only against learning any thing from the physicians, but against even appearing to have learned this art. Nevertheless, appoint me to be your physician; and I will do my best to learn by experimenting upon you."—XEN. *Mem.* IV. ii. 5.

NOTE 25, p. 24.

To account for this identification of politics with virtue, we must remember that to the Greek the art of politics comprised all excellence. To him the state was the moral and religious law in one, a community in good living, its end being the full and harmonious development of human nature in the citizen; or, in other words, the unimpeded activity of his moral and intellectual power to work,— of his "excellence" or virtue. For if we examine the virtues in the exercise of which this "good living" consists, we shall find that they all imply social relations, and that thus the individual who realises his chief good or happiness is necessarily a citizen, — what is meant by citizenship being, not the mere possession of civil rights, but the becoming a part of the state, the living its life. Thus, ruling and being ruled, a man exercises not only the virtues of obedience, not only the common moral virtues, but also the excellences of moral wisdom and command: his life is pre-eminently one of virtue. See "*Hellenica*," *Essay on Aristotle's Conception of the State*, by A. C. Bradley, M.A.

NOTE 26, p. 24.

The allusion is to the sacred flocks, who, being dedicated to the gods, were exempted from work and allowed to range at will in what may be called the "glebe" or land belonging to the temple. This notion was familiar to the Greeks from Homer's description of the catastrophe which Odysseus' men brought about by their impious slaughter of the sacred sheep and cattle of the sun (*Odyssey*, xii. 127-141). Herodotus also (ix. 93), in speaking of the Corinthian colony Apollonia in Epirus, says, "In this town there are likewise herds of cattle sacred to Helios. In the daytime they feed by the side of the river. ... During the night men who are elected from amongst the citizens as conspicuous for their wealth and lineage take turns in watching over them, each one for a year's length."

NOTE 27, p. 25.

ALCIBIADES and CLEINIAS were distant cousins of Pericles and his brother Ariphron. Alcibiades, in one of the two dialogues bearing his name, which are somewhat doubtfully attributed to Plato, remarks that the ill-success of Pericles in the education of his sons and Cleinias does not detract from his wisdom; for the former were born simpletons, and the latter was a madman, which epithet is explained by one of the scholiasts as meaning that Cleinias was too obstinate to take any one's advice.

NOTE 28, p. 26.

The history to be related is foreshadowed in the names of these Titan brothers, the significations of which are *Forethought* and *Afterthought*.

NOTE 29, p. 28.

It is hardly necessary to state that the Latin divinities corresponding to this god and goddess are Vulcan and Minerva, and that Hermes, who appears in the latter part of the myth, is the Roman Mercury. With the change of name which followed upon the transplanting of Greek divinities to Roman soil, a corresponding transformation was brought about in their character. If we would see them divested of the Roman mask under which they have too long been travestied, and assume again their Greek features, the old names must be restored under which they were called into existence by the Hellenes, that pliant and mobile race, the creations of whose graceful fancy the unimaginative Romans could but imitate, and, in so doing, vulgarise. (See preface to *Les Deux Masques*, by Paul de Saint Victor.)

NOTE 30, p. 28.

In Hesiod's version of this story (*Theogony*, 534–537), PROMETHEUS is punished,—

"Because he had striven in counsel with Zeus the almighty,
And practised deception against the dread son of old Cronos,"

the deception consisting, not in any benefactions wrought for mankind, but in the unequal division, at a sacrifice, of a 'slaughtered ox.'

His punishment is described as follows:—

"Prometheus the wily he punished with bondage most grievous,
And fast to a pillar in strong-riven bonds him enchained;
And he sent forth an eagle upon him with pinions wide spreading,
To prey on his liver forever renewed for the feeding;
Since what by the broad-winged bird every day was consumed
Grew again, by each night for each morrow made good and restored."
— Hes. *Theogony*, 521–525.

Aeschylus gives no special prominence to the deceit of Prometheus, but represents him as a martyr in the cause of man, of whom Zeus, as he bitterly complains,—

"Took no heed, but purposed utterly
To crush their race and plant another new;
And, I excepted, none dared cross his will;
But I did dare, and mortal man I freed
From passing thunderstricken on to Hades' depths;
And therefore am I bound beneath these woes
Dreadful to suffer, pitiable to see:
And I, who in my pity thought of men
More than myself, have not been worthy deemed
To gain like favour; but all ruthlessly
I thus am chained, foul shame this sight to Zeus."
—*Prom. vinct.* 239–249. [Plumptre's translation.

Note 31, p. 28.

The clause 'on account of his kinship with the gods' which occurs here in the Greek MSS. so mars the sense of this passage that some of the editors suppose it to be by a later hand and enclose it in brackets. Accordingly in this translation it has not been retained.

Note 32, p. 38.

The authenticity of the additional clause 'as is proved by their committing injustice' which occurs in the text has also been questioned, and it is here omitted as interfering with the connection of thought.

Note 33, p. 42.

The length of the "long course," from the starting-point to the farther goal and back, was twenty-four *stadia* (about three miles).

That the professional runners who were employed for special emergencies were trained to wonderful speed is shown by the story of the Plataean Euchidas, who, on being sent after the battle of Salamis to fetch fire from Apollo's altar, made in one day the distance between Plataea and Delphi and back,—a thousand *stadia* (about a hundred miles). The exertion, however, cost him his life.

Note 34, p. 45.

The PRYTANEIUM was a large hall where the prytanes (see note 23, p. 24) transacted their business, and dined at a common table, maintained at public expense for them, for guests of the city, and for certain citizens to whom this honour was awarded in return for distinguished services to the country.

Note 35, p. 47.

SIMONIDES, the author of this ode, was a native of the island of Ceos. He cultivated all styles of poetry, but particularly excelled in epigrams, of which some hundred remain. In the ode in question, which was written to celebrate a chariot victory of Scopas one of the tyrants of Thessaly, Simonides, to avoid censure for awarding open praise to a tyrant, dwells upon a saying of Pittacus to the effect that it is hardly possible for men to be good, and declares that since it is useless to war against the impossible, they who are not absolutely vicious are worthy of respect and honour. Scopas, far from satisfied by this generalisation, withheld from Simonides the half of his payment, bidding him seek the rest at the hands of the Dioscuri (Castor and Pollux), with whose eulogy the ode ended. Their reward was not long in forthcoming. Shortly after, as the poet sat at table with Scopas and his guests he received an urgent summons in obedience to which he left the building and no sooner had he done so than the walls fell, burying all within. The bodies of the dead were recognised only by the help of Simonides, whose memory enabled him to recollect the place of each guest at the table. This anecdote, which is at least *ben trovato*, accounts for a tradition that Simonides was the inventor of the art of mnemonics.

NOTE 36, p. 47.

PITTACUS of Mitylene in Lesbos, who, like many others, was classed among the seven wise men of Greece, played an important part in the history of his native city. His services were rewarded by his appointment as governor, in which capacity he ruled with the greatest moderation and sagacity. One of the laws attributed to him was that any fault committed under the influence of wine should receive double punishment. His practical wisdom was shown no less by his pithy sayings than by his political sagacity.

NOTE 37, p. 48.

This quotation is from Hesiod's *Works and Days* (285 fol.). Compare Matt. vii. 14: "Strait is the gate and narrow is the way which leadeth unto life."

Note 38, p. 51.

In the *Symposium*, 220 A, Alcibiades tells us that Socrates, at Potidaea, "although he did not care to drink, yet when constrained to do so outdid everybody else; and, most wonderful of all, no man had ever beheld Socrates drunk."

Note 39, p. 52.

This reference is to the passage where Diomede, on volunteering to visit the Trojan camp as a spy, asks that a companion may go with him.

> " My heart and the spirit of valiance within me, O Nestor
> Is prompted to enter the lines of the foeman hard by us, —
> The Trojan's; but now, if some comrade will join and go with me,
> More spirit and comforting warmth shall there be in the venture.
> Let two go together, and one understands ere the other
> How gain shall be compassed; alone, even well understanding,
> Yet one man in forethought is scant, and of flimsy devices."
> —*Iliad*, 220–229.

Note 40, p. 56.

This passage has been variously interpreted, and the want of logic no less than of candour displayed in the argument by both interlocutors makes the drift of their statements somewhat problematic. Plainly put, the case would seem to stand as follows:—

The admission of Protagoras, to the effect that the confidence derived from knowledge is a predicate of courage, supposes the *union* of courage and knowledge, and is therefore a step towards the *identification* of the two,—that being the end which Socrates has in view. But the attempt of Socrates to prove an *absolute* identification through the assumption of an ungranted premise, gives Protagoras an excuse for escaping from his previous assertion of the absolute independence of courage and knowledge, and for advancing a new proposition, that courage in the soul is like strength in the body, the result partly of nature and partly of training.

At this juncture, we should expect Socrates to maintain afresh that the distinctive mark of courage, that which makes it other than pure recklessness, is an intimate knowledge of the dangers which it must confront, since only when possessed of this knowledge may a man "unarmed, face dangers with a heart of trust," and to urge on new grounds the absolute identification of this knowledge with courage. That Socrates instead of urging this point should, as he does, abruptly shift his ground and adopt another line of attack, implies a tacit though tardy recognition of the truth contained in the last proposition of Protagoras.

The identification of knowledge and virtue was a favourite doctrine with Socrates, and it constantly recurs in the dialogues of Plato, though often in a modified form. In the *Republic* (429 C-430 C), the lawless daring of the wild beast and the slave, which has nothing to do with education, is spoken of as unworthy to be called by the name of courage. We read there, that, as the dyer is at great pains to prepare the white ground which best receives and longest retains all other dyes, so the wise man, by right education, prepares the soul to receive and retain the dye of the laws and of right convictions concerning dangers and all other matters, that thus no lye, such as pleasure or fear or pain, which may come thereafter, may have any power to wash it away.

"Ethical virtue," says Aristotle (*Nicomachean Ethics*, B. VI. c. 2), "is a habit informed by purpose, and purpose is impulse guided by deliberate choice. If, therefore, the purpose is to be worthy, the principle must be true and the impulse right; whatever is affirmed by the one, the other must pursue." Here we see both sides of the truth in their relation to each other. In the union of impulse and reason all virtue is comprised; only in the light of practical wisdom, which alone can point out the end to be striven for, does virtue unfold itself.

NOTES ON THE REPUBLIC.

NOTE 41, p. 65.

THE PEIRAEUS was the chief port of Athens. It was the ome of the *metics* — this term including all resident Greeks not of Athenian parentage — and of the foreign residents, as at this day are the ports of Galata and Pera in Constantinople.

NOTE 42, p. 65.

Plato and his two brothers, GLAUCON and ADEIMANTUS, claimed descent on their father's side from Codrus, the last king of Athens; while through their mother, Perictione, they were nephews of Critias, the leader of the violent faction of the Thirty Tyrants, and were also connected with the great law-giver Solon. Glaucon is said to have written a number of dialogues, none of which, however, are extant. A conversation between him and Socrates is given in the *Memorabilia* of Xenophon (iii. 6) in which Glaucon is cured of a wild ambition to put himself at the head of public affairs, by being led to perceive and acknowledge his own ignorance and incapacity.

ADEIMANTUS, who is shortly to be introduced, is known to us only by the representation of him in the *Republic*.

NOTE 43, p. 65.

The worship of BENDIS, the Thracian Artemis, was first celebrated in Athens by a public festival at the time when Plato represents this dialogue as opening.

Note 44, p. 65.

POLEMARCHUS and his younger brother LYSIAS subsequently joined the Athenian colony which had been sent by Pericles to found Thurii, a city in the southern part of Italy, or Magna Grecia. Here the two brothers remained until the disturbances which followed the failure of the Athenian expedition against Syracuse compelled their return to Athens. They there founded a manufactory of shields, and amassed a large fortune which excited the cupidity of the Thirty Tyrants. Without accusation or trial, Polemarchus was sentenced to drink the hemlock, while Lysias only escaped with his life by fleeing to Megara. The oration which, upon his return to Athens, he pronounced against Eratosthenes in order to avenge his brother's death, gave him great reputation; and he was able to retrieve his fortune by carrying on a school of oratory, but principally by the speeches which he wrote to be delivered in the law-courts by his clients, on their own behalf. Of these he is said to have written no less than four hundred and twenty-five, of which however one hundred and ninety-two were believed to be spurious.

Note 45, p. 66.

The riches of NICERATUS rendered him also a victim of the Thirty. He is said to have taken a deep interest in literary matters, and to have known by heart so much of Homer that upon one occasion he held a contest with certain rhapsodists, — men whose profession it was to recite verses publicly, especially those of Homer. But he is best known as the son of Nicias, whose career, characterised by its patriotism and successful generalship during the early part of the Peloponnesian war, had the disastrous ending which Browning has summed up in these words : —

> " When poor, reluctant Nicias, pushed by fate,
> Went falteringly against Syracuse,
> And there shamed Athens, lost her ships and men,
> And gained a grave, or death without a grave."
> —*Balaustion's Adventure.*

Note 46, p. 66.

The closing line in the following passage from Lucretius is an evident allusion to this feature of the Athenian Bendideia:—

"The sum of all things always thus renews,
And man lends man the borrowed life men use;
Some races wane, while others wax more strong;
Changed in brief time all kinds through life that throng
Shall all like runners pass life's torch along."

— *De R. N.* II., 45-79.

Note 47, p. 67.

For LYSIAS see note 44.

THRASYMACHUS was a famous teacher of rhetoric, his style being regarded as a happy medium between the flowery eloquence of Gorgias and the simple directness of Lysias. Grote thinks that he is here misrepresented by Plato; but the account of him given in the *Republic* is confirmed by Aristotle's allusion (*Rhet.* III., 1413 a. 8) to his jeers at Niceratus on the occasion of his defeat in the contest above mentioned (note 45), and also by a pun upon the name of Thrasymachus, made to ridicule his contentiousness (*Rhet.* II., 1400 b. 20). In the *Phædrus* he is nicknamed the "rhetorical giant of Chalcedon."

Of EUTHYDEMUS, CHARMANTIDES, and CLEITOPHON nothing is known.

Note 48, p. 67.

CEPHALUS was a native of Syracuse, who, at the instance of his friend Pericles, had taken up his abode in the Peiraeus, the foreign quarter of Athens. Lysias, in the celebrated speech above mentioned, alludes to the fact that three houses were at this time owned by the family, and we have other evidence of the ease and prosperity which surrounded its members.

Note 49, p. 67.

Acts of private worship amongst the Greeks may be classed under three heads:—

A. Those which involved ceremonies of a special nature,

being connected with certain divinities who were patrons of certain families, races, or trades.

B. Those which had to do with family events, as marriages, births, and deaths.

C. Those which were binding upon every God-fearing man in his own house, and of which domestic sacrifices, such as Cephalus is about to make, formed a chief part. Of these Hesiod speaks when he says (*Works and Days*, v.v. 335–339), —

> "The rites to the utmost fulfil of the gods everlasting,
> Be holy and pure: thou shalt burn richest thighs as thine offering,
> And oft with libations and incense propitiate Heaven,
> When darkness prompts thee to sleep, as when sun-dawn awakes thee."

Before paying homage to other gods, an appeal was made to Hestia, whose holy place was the family hearth, and often also to Zeus Ephestios, the protector of the home. Both of these divinities were connected with public as well as with private worship; while a third, Zeus Ktesios (the provider), was worshipped almost exclusively in private. The opinion given a little later by Cephalus as to the true value of riches has a peculiar appropriateness, if we imagine him as about to complete a thank-offering to Zeus Ktesios for the good gifts with which his family was so bountifully supplied.

Note 50, p. 68.

A Homeric phrase frequently met with in the poets. See *Iliad*, xxii. 60; *Odyssey*, xv. 348; Hesiod, *Works and Days*, 329.

Note 51, p. 68.

"Equals delight in equals" is Jowett's translation of the proverb here alluded to, which is quoted in the *Phædrus*, 240 C. It is meant, however, to apply only to equals in age.

Note 52, p. 70.

The island of SERIPHOS was one of the smallest and least important of the Cyclades.

Note 53, p. 70.

Cicero's treatise on old age (ii. and iii.) contains an almost literal translation of this passage. The question about the road which all must travel is asked by Laelius and is followed by Cato Major's answer,—an exact reproduction of that of Cephalus, with the single exception that the anecdote about Sophocles is reserved for later use (xiv). Laelius then asks the question about money, which receives the same answer as that given by Cephalus, neither anecdote nor comment being omitted.

Note 54, p. 72.

Fragments of *Pindar*, 198 [233]. Bergk's edition.

Note 55, p. 74.

On being criticised by his friend Atticus for having in the second and third books of the dialogue, called *De Oratore*, suppressed Scaevola, one of the prominent characters in the first book, Cicero writes: "I did exactly what Plato, our inspired master, has done in his *Republic*. For when Socrates first arrives at the house of Cephalus, his aged and cheerful host takes part in the discussion until the first topic of discourse is exhausted: then, as soon as he has comfortably said his own say, he declares that he must go to attend to the sacrifices; nor does he again appear. I believe that Plato thought it hardly proper to involve a man of his years in so protracted a discussion."—*Ad Att.* iv. xvi. a. 3.

Note 56, p. 75.

JUSTICE is here taken, not in its narrow meaning of simple *equity*, but in its broad scriptural sense of *righteousness*.

That justice—which embraces the whole duty of man—is essentially an art, is maintained by Aristotle, who asserts that, even more than other arts, it requires the most practiced skill to be brought to perfection. Thus he says (*Nic. Ethics*, I. p. 1101, 1–5 a.), —

" We believe that the truly good and sensible man bears all fortunes with dignity, and always makes the best of whatever falls to his lot; just as a good general uses the army ready to his hand so as best to fulfil the purposes of war, and as the shoemaker makes the best shoe out of the leather that has been given him."

NOTE 57, p. 76.

This quotation is from the passage descriptive of the visit paid by Odysseus to

"Autolycus, sire of his mother, who greatly exceeded
All men both in falsehood and thieving, — a god gave the gift,
Even Hermes himself; of lambs and of kids, grateful offerings,
The thigh-bones he burned; and the god, not displeased, sent his help."
— *Odyssey*, xix. 395-398.

NOTE 58, p. 78.

The tradition was, that, on meeting a wolf, the man must be the first to catch the beast's eye, otherwise he would be struck dumb.

NOTE 59, p. 79.

" Verbal irony may be described as a figure which enables the speaker to convey his meaning with greater force, by means of a contrast between his thought and his expression, or, to speak more accurately, between the thought which he evidently designs to express, and that which his words properly signify. . . . There is, however, an irony which deserves to be distinguished from the ordinary species by a different name, and which may be properly called *dialectic irony*. . . . The writer effects his purpose by placing the opinion of his adversary in the foreground, and saluting it with every demonstration of respect, while he is busied in withdrawing, one by one, all the supports on which it rests; and he never ceases to approach it with an air of deference, until he has completely undermined it, when he leaves it to sink by the weight of its own absurdity." — Thirlwall's *Irony of Sophocles*. Philological Museum, Cambridge, 1833.

Note 60, p. 86.

This proverb was used to ridicule those who undertook what was beyond their strength.

Note 61, p. 93.

In emphasising this reason as an inducement to enter public life, Socrates appeals to a lower motive than he usually seeks to arouse in his hearers. Thus, in a conversation with Aristippus in which he sets forth the duty of assuming offices of responsibility, Socrates, in speaking of those "who labour that they may gain strength both of body and of mind, and that they may govern their own household well, and perform kindnesses for their friends and services for their country," asks how it can be imagined, that, "with such objects in view, these men will not labour with all gladness and lead a life of true delight, well content with themselves, and receiving the praise and admiration of other men?"—XEN. *Mem.* II. i. 19.

Note 62, p. 107.

"There is a just man that perisheth in his righteousness, and there is a wicked man that prolongeth his life in his wickedness."—*Eccles.* vii. 15.

Note 63, p. 108.

The allusion is to the character of Amphiaraus as described by Aeschylus in the *Seven against Thebes*, from which these lines are quoted:—

> "On his rounded shield no blazon could men find,
> Best to be, not seem, he makes his life's pursuit,
> Garnering from the deep-spread plough-lands of his mind,
> Harvests rich in wholesome wisdom's ripened fruit.
> Send, I charge, against him, rowers bold and skilled,
> Feared of men is he whom fear of God hath filled."
>
> —v.v. 587–592

"In some of the MSS., the word 'just' stands in place of 'best' [in line 588], and the story runs that when the play was first represented, the actor who was speaking the part and the whole audience looked towards Aristides 'the just,' to whom alone they felt that the description was applicable."— Plutarch, *Aristides, ch. 3*.

NOTE 64, p. 112.

"The labour of the righteous tendeth to life: the fruit of the wicked to sin." — *Prov.* x. 16.

NOTE 65, p. 114.

This name was first given to a mournful song with flute accompaniment, which seems originally to have been brought from Asia Minor, but it was finally applied to a particular kind of metre whenever used, quite irrespective of the subject. Always, however, it is the expression of the poet's own personal feelings in contradistinction to the impersonal character which belongs to epic poetry.

NOTE 66, p. 114.

As we do not know what date to assign to this dialogue, it is uncertain which of the many battles fought at Megara is here meant.

MANUAL OF MYTHOLOGY

FOR THE USE OF

SCHOOLS, ART STUDENTS AND GENERAL READERS,

FOUNDED ON THE WORKS OF PETISCUS, PRELLER, AND WELCKER.

By ALEXANDER S. MURRAY,

Department of Greek and Roman Antiquities, British Museum.

With 45 Plates on tinted paper. representing more than 90 Mythological Subjects.

REPRINTED FROM THE SECOND REVISED LONDON EDITION.

One volume, crown 8vo, $2.25.

There has long been needed a compact, manageable Manual of Mythology, which should be a guide to the Art student and the general reader, and at the same time answer the purposes of a school text-book. This volume which has been prepared by the Director of the Department of Greek and Roman Antiquities in the British Museum, upon the basis of the works of Petiscus, Preller, and Welcker, has had so extensive a sale in the English edition, as to prove that it precisely supplies this want. This American edition has been reprinted from the latest English edition, and contains all the illustrations of the latter, *while the chapter upon Eastern Mythology has been carefully revised by Prof. W. D. Whitney, of Yale College.*

N. B.—Teachers wishing to examine this work with a view to introducing it as a text-book, will have it sent to them, by forwarding their address and $1.35.

*** *The above book for sale by all booksellers, or will be sent, post or express charge is paid, upon receipt of the price by the publishers,*

CHARLES SCRIBNER'S SONS,
743 AND 745 BROADWAY, NEW YORK.

SOCRATES:

A Translation of the Apology, Crito, and parts of the Phædo of Plato, containing the Defence of Socrates at his Trial, his Conversations in Prison, with his Thoughts on the Future Life, and an Account of his Death. With an Introduction by Professor W. W. GOODWIN of Harvard College.

A New and Cheaper Edition. Paper Covers. Price, 50 cts.

Four years ago, the literary world was surprised and delighted by the appearance of a new translation, by an unknown hand, of some of Plato's immortal masterpieces, which was at once pronounced by scholars far superior to any ever before given to English readers. The costliness of the elegant little volume, though it seemed an appropriate setting to the gems it contained, put it beyond the reach of the masses of the people and so hindered its chief object. It has now been issued in a new, cheaper, but still very attractive edition, which will bring within the means of every reader, an acquaintance with the great philosopher and his greater master,

[*From the Boston Courier.*]

"This book is a most valuable addition to the useful literature of the day. It will give those unacquainted with Greek a very clear idea of the writings of Plato, and of the character and teachings of his master. The translation, although not claiming to be literal, could hardly be bettered, and the words of the philosopher are clothed in the purest, simplest, and most expressive English. Rarely has a work been translated from the Greek that has so faithfully preserved the spirit of the original. Professor Goodwin was right in thinking that this volume would be welcomed by many to whom Plato and Socrates had hitherto been only venerated names, and the translator is deserving of the warm thanks of all who have not had the advantage of what is called a liberal education, for placing within their reach a volume that contains the essence of writings that the scholar has laboriously toiled after. It is a model translation in every respect, and one that can be easily read and understood. Some idea of the scope of the book may be obtained from the following extract from the admirable introduction by the professor of Greek at Harvard College : 'The Apology giving Plato's report of the memorable defence which he had heard from his master's lips in the Athenian court shows the eccentric but sturdy independence of Socrates, the inflexible resolution with which he executed what he believed to be a divine command, and the calm fearlessness with which he announced to the court that he should obey God rather than man, and that no human power should compel him to desert his post. It also gives an amusing account of the manner in which Socrates went about exposing ignorance and convicting imposture. The Crito gives an opposite but no less striking view of the character of Socrates, showing the real respect for the laws and institutions of his country, which he felt under all his defiant independence. . . . In the Phædo we have the effective narrative of the closing scene of the life of Socrates, with the conversation on the soul and immortality, which Plato represents him as holding with his friends during the few last hours before he drank the hemlock.'"

*** *For Sale by all booksellers, or sent, by mail, upon receipt of price, by*
CHARLES SCRIBNER'S SONS, PUBLISHERS,
743 AND 745 BROADWAY, NEW YORK.

SOCRATES:

CRITICAL NOTICES.

From the N. E. Journal of Education.

"As educators, and interested in general popular culture, we are very glad that the Messrs. Scribner have now wisely brought this delightful little book within reach of all readers. Its first appearance, in more costly form, four years ago, was a sensation in the literary world. The unknown translator—now known to be a lady—took rank at once among the best interpreters of these immortal dialogues to English readers, whether for grasp of the original, or strength and beauty of English.

"As many more will read this second edition than had access to the first, we will briefly review some of its excellencies, with the desire especially of calling the attention of teachers to its admirable adaptation to use in schools and classes of literature."

From the N. Y. Evening Post.

"The translation is supremely good, rendering the original into pure, simple, direct and lucid English, not absolutely literal, and yet so nearly so that only a careful comparison with the Greek reveals its departures from exact literalness; and these departures are uniformly in the interest of perspicuousness and simplicity in the English idiom. We do not at the moment remember any translation of a Greek author which is a better specimen of idiomatic English than this, or a more faithful rendering of the real spirit of the original into English as good and as simple as the Greek. . . . Such a translation as he here offers makes the reading of the original well nigh superfluous. His English text is Greek in its strength and nervous energy, and it carries with it much of the charm of the original."

From the N. Y. Observer.

"There are even yet many people, no doubt, to whom Plato is an unknown writer, and who have never read the wonderful defence of Socrates before his judges, or the still more remarkable account of his last hours and death. We envy such the pleasure of reading this little volume and making the acquaintance of that one, who, of all the heathen philosophers, most nearly apprehended the spirit of Christianity and " the power of an endless life."

From the Chicago Tribune.

"The fragments embodied in this little book are stamped with such greatness and purity as the world has seldom seen, even in its most favored centuries. The public owes a debt of gratitude for such a work, both to translator and publisher."

From the New York Times.

"We have carefully compared the present translations with Jowett's, Whewell's Victor Cousin's and others, and they seem to us to convey more of the original tone of the Greek, and at the same time to be more in harmony with modern style than any of these famous versions.

₊ *For Sale by all booksellers, or sent, post-paid, upon receipt of price, by*

CHARLES SCRIBNER'S SONS, PUBLISHERS,

743 AND 745 BROADWAY, NEW YORK.

[OVER.

A New Edition, Library Style.

The History of Greece.

By Prof. Dr. ERNST CURTIUS.

Translated by ADOLPHUS WILLIAM WARD, M. A., Fellow of St. Peter's College, Cambridge, Prof. of History in Owen's College, Manchester.

UNIFORM WITH MOMMSEN'S HISTORY OF ROME.

Five volumes, crown 8vo, gilt top.   ·   Price per set, $10.00.

Curtius's *History of Greece* is similar in plan and purpose to Mommsen's *History of Rome*, with which it deserves to rank in every respect as one of the great masterpieces of historical literature. Avoiding the minute details which overburden other similar works, it groups together in a very picturesque manner all the important events in the history of this kingdom, which has exercised such a wonderful influence upon the world's civilization. The narrative of Prof. Curtius's work is flowing and animated, and the generalizations, although bold, are philosophical and sound.

CRITICAL NOTICES.

"Professor Curtius's eminent scholarship is a sufficient guarantee for the trustworthiness of his history, while the skill with which he groups his facts, and his effective mode of narrating them, combine to render it no less readable than sound. Prof. Curtius everywhere maintains the true dignity and impartiality of history, and it is evident his sympathies are on the side of justice, humanity, and progress." — *London Athenæum.*

"We cannot express our opinion of Dr. Curtius's book better than by saying that it may be fitly ranked with Theodor Mommsen's great work." — *London Spectator.*

"As an introduction to the study of Grecian history, no previous work is comparable to the present for vivacity and picturesque beauty, while in sound learning and accuracy of statement it is not inferior to the elaborate productions which enrich the literature of the age." — *N. Y. Daily Tribune.*

"The History of Greece is treated by Dr. Curtius so broadly and freely in the spirit of the nineteenth century, that it becomes in his hands one of the worthiest and most instructive branches of study for all who desire something more than a knowledge of isolated facts for their education. This translation ought to become a regular part of the accepted course of reading for young men at college, and for all who are in training for the free political life of our country." — *N. Y. Evening Post.*

CHARLES SCRIBNER'S SONS, PUBLISHERS,

743 AND 745 BROADWAY, NEW YORK.

A New Edition, Library Style.

The History of Rome,

FROM THE EARLIEST TIME TO THE PERIOD OF ITS DECLINE.

By Dr. THEODOR MOMMSEN.

Translated, with the author's sanction and additions, by the Rev. W. P. DICKSON, Regius Professor of Biblical Criticism in the University of Glasgow, late Classical Examiner of the University of St. Andrews. With an introduction by Dr. LEONHARD SCHMITZ, and a copious Index of the whole four volumes, prepared especially for this edition.

REPRINTED FROM THE REVISED LONDON EDITION.

Four Volumes, crown 8vo, gilt top.　　　　　　　　　Price per Set, $8.00.

DR. MOMMSEN has long been known and appreciated through his researches into the languages, laws, and institutions of Ancient Rome and Italy, as the most thoroughly versed scholar now living in these departments of historical investigation. To a wonderfully exact and exhaustive knowledge of these subjects, he unites great powers of generalization, a vigorous, spirited, and exceedingly graphic style and keen analytical powers, which give this history a degree of interest and a permanent value possessed by no other record of the decline and fall of the Roman Commonwealth. "Dr. Mommsen's work," as Dr. Schmitz remarks in the introduction, "though the production of a man of most profound and extensive learning and knowledge of the world, is not as much designed for the professional scholar as for intelligent readers of all classes who take an interest in the history of by-gone ages, and are inclined there to seek information that may guide them safely through the perplexing mazes of modern history."

CRITICAL NOTICES.

"A work of the very highest merit; its learning is exact and profound; its narrative full of genius and skill; its descriptions of men are admirably vivid. We wish to place on record our opinion that Dr. Mommsen's is by far the best history of the Decline and Fall of the Roman Commonwealth." — *London Times.*

"This is the best history of the Roman Republic, taking the work on the whole — the author's complete mastery of his subject, the variety of his gifts and acquirements, his graphic power in the delineation of national and individual character, and the vivid interest which he inspires in every portion of his book. He is without an equal in his own sphere." — *Edinburgh Review.*

CHARLES SCRIBNER'S SONS, PUBLISHERS,

743 AND 745 BROADWAY, NEW YORK.

The Religions of the Ancient World

Including Egypt, Assyria and Babylonia, Persia, India, Phœnicia, Etruria, Greece, Rome.

By GEORGE RAWLINSON, M.A.

One Volume, 12mo, - - - - $1.00.
Uniform with "The Origin of Nations."

Canon Rawlinson's great learning and his frequent contributions to the history of ancient nations qualify him to treat the subject of this volume with a breadth of view and accuracy of knowledge that few other writers can lay claim to. The treatise is not intended to give an exhaustive review of ancient religions, but to enable the students of history to form a more accurate apprehension of the inner life of the ancient world.

"The historical studies which have elevated this author's works to the highest position have made him familiar with those beliefs which once directed the world's thought; and he has done literature no better service than in this little volume. . . . The book is, then, to be accepted as a sketch, and as the most trustworthy sketch in our language, of the religions discussed."—*N. Y. Christian Advocate.*

THE ORIGIN OF NATIONS

By Professor GEORGE RAWLINSON, M.A.

One Volume, 12mo. With maps, - - $1.00.

The first part of this book, Early Civilizations, discusses the antiquity of civilization in Egypt and the other early nations of the East. The second part, Ethnic Affinities in the Ancient World, is an examination of the ethnology of Genesis, showing its accordance with the latest results of modern ethnographical science.

"An attractive volume, which is well worthy of the careful consideration of every reader."—*Observer.*

"A work of genuine scholarly excellence and a useful offset to a great deal of the superficial current literature on such subjects."
—*Congregationalist.*

"Dr. Rawlinson brings to this discussion long and patient research, a vast knowledge and intimate acquaintance with what has been written on both sides of the question."—*Brooklyn Union-Argus.*

For Sale by all booksellers, or sent, post-paid, upon receipt of price, by
CHARLES SCRIBNER'S SONS, PUBLISHERS,
743 AND 745 BROADWAY, NEW YORK.

THE BEGINNINGS OF HISTORY

According to the Bible and the Traditions of the Oriental Peoples. From the Creation of Man to the Deluge. By FRANCOIS LENORMANT, Professor of Archæology at the National Library of France, etc. (Translated from the Second French Edition). With an introduction by FRANCIS BROWN, Associate Professor in Biblical Philology, Union Theological Seminary.

1 Vol., 12mo, 600 pages, - - - *$2.50.*

"What should we see in the first chapters of Genesis?" writes M. Lenormant in his preface—"A revealed narrative, or a human tradition, gathered up for preservation by inspired writers as the oldest memory of their race? This is the problem which I have been led to examine by comparing the narrative of the Bible with those which were current among the civilized peoples of most ancient origin by which Israel was surrounded, and from the midst of which it came."

The book is not more erudite than it is absorbing in its interest. It has had an immense influence upon contemporary thought; and has approached its task with an unusual mingling of the reverent and the scientific spirit.

"That the 'Oriental Peoples' had legends on the Creation, the Fall of Man, the Deluge, and other primitive events, there is no denying. Nor is there any need of denying it, as this admirable volume shows. Mr. Lenormant is not only a believer in revelation, but a devout confessor of what came by Moses; as well as of what came by Christ. In this explanation of Chaldean, Babylonian, Assyrian and Phenician tradition, he discloses a prodigality of thought and skill allied to great variety of pursuit, and diligent manipulation of what he has secured. He 'spoils the Egyptians' by boldly using for Christian purposes materials, which, if left unused, might be turned against the credibility of the Mosaic records.

"From the mass of tradition here examined it would seem that if these ancient legends have a common basis of truth, the first part of Genesis stands more generally related to the religious history of mankind, than if it is taken primarily as one account, by one man, to one people. . . . While not claiming for the author the setting forth of the absolute truth, nor the drawing from what he has set forth the soundest conclusions, we can assure our readers of a diminishing fear of learned unbelief after the perusal of this work."—*The New Englander.*

"With reference to the book as a whole it may be said: (1). That nowhere else can one obtain the mass of information upon this subject in so convenient a form; (2). That the investigation is conducted in a truly scientific manner, and with an eminently Christian spirit; (3). That the results, though very different from those in common acceptance, contain much that is interesting and to say the least, plausible; (4). That the author while he seems in a number of cases to be injudicious in his statements and conclusions, has done work in investigation and in working out details that will be of service to all, whether general readers or specialists."—*The Hebrew Student.*

"The work is one that deserves to be studied by all students of ancient history, and in particular by ministers of the Gospel, whose office requires them to interpret the Scriptures, and who ought not to be ignorant of the latest and most interesting contribution of science to the elucidation to the sacred volume."—*New York Tribune.*

** *For Sale by all booksellers, or sent, post-paid, upon receipt of price,*

CHARLES SCRIBNER'S SONS, PUBLISHERS,
743 AND 745 BROADWAY, NEW YORK.

A MONUMENT OF MODERN SCHOLARSHIP.

THE DIALOGUES OF PLATO.

TRANSLATED INTO ENGLISH, WITH ANALYSIS AND INTRODUCTIONS,

BY B. JOWETT, M.A.,

MASTER OF BALLIOL COLLEGE, OXFORD, AND REGIUS PROFESSOR OF GREEK.

A NEW AND CHEAPER EDITION.

Four Volumes, Crown 8vo, $8.00 per Set, in Cloth.

By this reduction in price, the well-known translation of Plato's Dialogues, by Professor Jowett, is to be brought more generally within the reach of students and others.

From the New York Tribune.

"The present work of Professor Jowett will be welcomed with profound interest, as the only adequate endeavor to transport the most precious monument of Grecian thought among the familiar treasures of English literature. The noble reputation of Professor Jowett, both as a thinker and a scholar, it may be premised, however, is a valid guaranty for the excellence of his performance. He is known as one of the most hard-working students of the English universities, in the departments of philology and criticism, whose exemplary diligence is fully equalled by his singular acuteness of penetration, his clear and temperate judgment, and his rare and absolute fidelity to the interests of truth."

PLATO'S BEST THOUGHTS.

AS COMPILED FROM PROFESSOR JOWETT'S TRANSLATION OF THE DIALOGUES OF PLATO.

BY REV. C. H. A. BULKLEY.

A NEW EDITION. PRICE REDUCED TO $1.50.

One Volume, Crown 8vo.

"This volume makes the best things in Plato accessible and available, and its index gives it the character of a dictionary." — *The Evangelist.*

⁂ Sent, postpaid, on receipt of price by the Publishers,

CHARLES SCRIBNER'S SONS,

743 AND 745 BROADWAY, NEW YORK.

www.ingramcontent.com/pod-product-compliance
Lightning Source LLC
Chambersburg PA
CBHW032156160426

43197CB00008B/943